Sweet Lemonade

When Life Serves You Lemons Make Lemonade

ACHIEVE THE LIFE YOU WANT...

Your Guide to:
Lasting Joy, Peace, Satisfying Relationships,
Financial Security and
A Rewarding Life

LaWanda Hill

Copyright © 2016 LaWanda Hill. All rights reserved. No portion of this book may be reproduced mechanically, electronically, or by any other means, including photocopying, without written permission of the publisher. It is illegal to copy this book, post it to a website, or distribute it by any other means without permission from the publisher.

LaWanda Hill
15524 Old Hammond Hwy.
Baton Rouge, LA 70816
lhill@lawandahill.com
www.lawandahill.com

Book design by Velin@Perseus-Design.com

Vector Design by Freepik.com

ISBN: 978-0-9970578-1-2

Limits of Liability and Disclaimer of Warranty
The author and publisher shall not be liable for your misuse of this material. This book is strictly for informational and educational purposes.

Warning – Disclaimer
The purpose of this book is to educate and entertain. The author and/or publisher do not guarantee that anyone following these techniques, suggestions, tips, ideas, or strategies will become successful. The author and/or publisher shall have neither liability nor responsibility to anyone with respect to any loss or damage caused, or alleged to be caused, directly or indirectly by the information contained in this book.

Also by LaWanda Hill:
Women On Fire Academy
Women On Fire Inner Circle

Meet LaWanda online and receive free training at
www.WomenOnFireAcademy.com

Table of Contents

Prologue xi

Chapter One: Changing Your Mindset 1

Chapter Two: Fulfilling Purpose 13

Chapter Three: Spirituality 25

Chapter Four: Good Parenting 35

Chapter Five: Act like a Lady 45

Chapter Six: The Man 59

Chapter Seven: Managing Finances 73

Chapter Eight: Build Your House 101

Chapter Nine: Family Is Everything 133

Epilogue 147

Acknowledgements

My heartfelt gratitude goes to Christ, Who has transformed my life from darkness to light. Thank You for making Yourself known to me and trusting me with the vision that You have placed within my heart for people all around the world. Thank You for the life experiences that made this book possible. Thank You for loving me unconditionally even when I didn't know how to love myself.

This book is dedicated to my wonderful family, who has given me the experiences that I can share with the world and has allowed me to become the woman that I am today: My supporting husband, Darius, Mom, and Dad; My beautiful children, Bobby, Brittany, and Brandy. To my brothers, Louis, Lester, Jason and Deon, thank you. And to my friends who stayed close to me even with my crazy schedule; Jackie, Shriva, Terrica and Adrienne. Thank you all and I love you!

Therefore if any man be in Christ, he is a new creature: old things are passed away; behold, all things are become new.
2 Corinthians 5:17

Prologue

Cindy Matthew crumpled the flyer and threw it across the room.

"Dog it!" the pretty eighteen-year-old blonde said softly under her breath. "I wish that meddlesome old lady would find another civic cause.

From the time Cindy was twelve, Clarisse Caldwell, the prim, perfectly coiffed lady who lived next door to Cindy's parents' modest three-bedroom bungalow in New Orleans East Carrollton neighborhood had kept a close eye on Cindy's every move. From the second story bedroom window of Clarisse's century-old Victorian home, she missed nothing that was going on in Cindy's backyard. It was impossible for Cindy to crawl out her bedroom window without Clarisse noticing and reporting her late-night liaisons with her drug friends to Cindy's parents.

Of course, that got Cindy grounded. But, it hadn't stopped her. Short of locking her in her room or handcuffing her to the bed, Cindy's parents couldn't keep her prisoner in her own home.

After the police brought her home drunk and bedraggled, Cindy's parents had cleared out all the liquor from their liquor cabinet. Clarisse had suggested they attend A-A meetings as a family. Well, that merely meant that Cindy changed her drug of choice from alcohol to pot. She smiled at the recollection of her "science project" the year she turned her father's greenhouse into a pot growing operation.

But even with her excellent crop of top-grade pot, the highs wore off. Soon, Cindy was stealing and turning tricks to make meth money.

When the police arrested her for possession and soliciting, the ever-vigilant and resourceful Clarisse contacted her son-in-law at the DA's office and managed to get charges lowered to probation—if Cindy attended a six-week rehab program.

Clarisse just happened to know of an excellent private clinic where a bed had just miraculously opened up.

Six weeks in rehab had convinced Cindy that a life as a meth user was not pretty. Girls who had been users most of their lives looked like the walking dead. Their bodies were skeletons. Their hair was white. They were missing teeth and their vacant eyes stared out of the deep sockets in shrunken faces.

Cindy's parents heaved a sigh of relief when they brought their daughter home clean and sober. Cindy returned to school. But things had changed. Her drug friends were reluctant to believe she was no longer a user. Physical fights

PROLOGUE

broke out when Cindy's friends were sure she had ratted on them. The school administration suggested that—for Cindy's safety and the tone of the school—she should finish her final year of high school somewhere else.

That was fine with Cindy. She wanted nothing more to do with her loser friends and the other kids at school ostracized her. She was oh-so-willing to be rid of that school.

Clarisse-to-the-rescue (as Cindy's father had taken to calling their enterprising next-door neighbor) knew of a private girls' school nearby. The headmistress just happened to be Clarisse's girlhood friend. They would take Cindy mid-semester as a personal favor to Clarisse. The Matthews willingly dipped into their retirement savings and shelled out the exorbitant tuition, confident that Cindy would graduate and be in line for college entrance to a prestigious institution.

That's how Cindy found herself at Archbishop; the snooty all-girls school where she would finish her high school education—and become pregnant.

It seemed that adventure followed Cindy wherever she went. She had actually enrolled at Archbishop determined to study hard, keep her nose out of trouble, and get good grades. It was the least she could do after the merry chase on which she had led her parents for her teenage years! And for a few weeks she made good on her promise. Always a clever student in spite of her spotted past, Cindy was at the top of her class in most subjects.

But, that was before she met Duke McCormick. Duke's sister, Tiffany, was head of the cheerleading squad. When one of the girls broke her ankle during practice, the team was desperate to get a replacement fast. Since Cindy was the right height and build, and she had a background in gymnastics, she as pressed into service.

When her parents expressed reluctance at Cindy's time away from classes Miss Whipple, the headmistress, assured Cindy's parents that this would be a great way to fit in socially and being a "well rounded student" would be looked upon favorably by college admissions boards. Besides, Cindy's marks were excellent. She could keep up and still get ready for the Cheerleaders' National Competition, Miss Whipple insisted.

So, Cindy started attending practices in Tiffany's spacious backyard and Duke started taking a keen interest in practices. Their liaison in the pool cabana seemed fated. What didn't seem so well planned was the discovery that Cindy was pregnant. She missed the prom and graduation ceremonies. But she did emerge from Archbishop with a high school diploma and the knowledge that rich people could buy abortions and silence as easily as they purchased bread and milk.

Chapter One:
Changing Your Mindset

"That woman," Cindy groaned. "Why can't she stay out of my life?"

Frustrated, Cindy smoothed out the flyer and read:

> "Once your mindset changes, everything on the outside will change along with it."
> **~Steve Maraboli,** *Life, the Truth, and Being Free*

Cindy had no idea what a mindset was or who this Steve Maraboli was but she had a sinking feeling she was about to find out.

"This will be a good experience for Cindy," Clarisse had insisted. "Changing your mindset will open lots of possibilities for you. It will give you a chance to take a second look at yourself."

"Why would I do that?" asked Cindy.

"Because you have a lot of potential," Clarisse replied.

"Potential for what?" Cindy asked sarcastically. "I think we've all seen where my potential has taken me."

"Not so," argued Clarisse. "What we've seen is where youth, inexperience, and poor choices have taken you!"

So that's how Cindy found herself in a workshop on "Changing Your Mindset".

As the speaker, a petite blonde stepped up to the microphone the group of thirty-five participants scattered throughout Meeting Room G of The Lamplighter Inn grew quiet.

"Good evening everyone. Thanks for coming to our first session of "Changing Your Mindset" I'm Pamela Brown." As she started the PowerPoint presentation, Pamela read, "Developing the right mindset is really crucial to succeed in anything. When I was switching jobs, I knew the path I had to take and what I had to do to get where I wanted to be."

"I'll bet she did," muttered a voice beside her.

Cindy snorted.

"My intuition told me I had developed the right mindset," said Pamela brightly.

CHAPTER ONE: CHANGING YOUR MINDSET

What is a Mindset?

Flashed the second slide in Pamela's PowerPoint.

"I'm sure you came here with some preconceived ideas about the topic and what this workshop could do for you. I want you to form groups with the others who are wearing the same number on their name tag," Pamela instructed with false enthusiasm.

"Like we're expected to go around staring at each other's chests," Cindy mumbled.

"I've got a better idea," the voice beside her said. "We're both fives. Let's just wait here until the other fives find us."

"And what if they don't?" challenged Cindy.'

"Then we'll assume we're a group of two." The young man in the baseball cap and neon orange sneakers shrugged. "What are they gonna do? Kick us out?"

"I should be that lucky!" exclaimed Cindy.

"You here as part of your probation? By the way, I'm Glenn."

"Cindy. And no I'm not on probation. I had to go to rehab for that."

"Then how did you get hoodwinked into this?" asked Glenn.

"The old lady who lives next door to my parents convinced them that I'd benefit from a new mindset."

"What do you think she meant by that?" asked Glenn.

"She thinks I need an attitude adjustment," replied Cindy.

When Pamela noted that each of the groups seemed to be done talking she called them back to the third slide of her PowerPoint.

"Your mindset is the sum of your knowledge, including beliefs and thoughts about the world and yourself in it. It is your filter for information you get in and put out. So it determines how you receive and react to information." When the audience looked perplexed, Pamela went on.

For instance, if I said, 'Fire!' what's the first thought that would come into your mind?"

"Man! I'm out of work again," called a middle-aged man with an obvious toupee.

"Call 911," said a shy fortyish woman.

"Get the marshmallows!" said a bird-like twenty-something girl with blue hair.

"Duck and run," said Glenn.

"Good. It's cold in here," responded Cindy.

"Great everyone," said Pamela. "Why do you suppose we had so many different reactions?"

"Because we all have different mindsets!" exclaimed Cindy.

CHAPTER ONE: CHANGING YOUR MINDSET

"Right, Cindy," said Pamela. "We often talk about someone having 'the mindset of an entrepreneur' or 'the mindset for working with computers'. Having the right mindset for what you want to do or be in life is often the biggest factor."

"Well, if I have the mindset of a chef and my father wants me to be a lawyer, then what?" challenged Glenn.

"Good question, Glenn," said Pamela. "Developing the right mindset is a way of learning something new and getting the most relevant information. So if you want to be a mechanic, you attend classes and apprentice and get from those experiences the information you need to become a competent mechanic. You develop a set of beliefs or truths. This is your mindset."

"But what if I want to be a writer and no one believes I have what it takes to be one?" asked the timid blonde.

"If you believe 'I am a successful writer', you will act in that way," said Pam. "You may think that belief is a little out of reach, Carrie," admitted Pamela. "However I have found that adopting beliefs that seem slightly out of reach can be very powerful. It changes your mindset. When your mindset changes so does how you behave."

When everyone started to nod Pamela flashed the next slide:

How to Change Your Mindset

1. Get the Best Information Only

"Let's take Glenn's example. If he wants to be a successful chef, where is he going to go to find the very best information?"

"Chef school," said Cindy.

"A successful chef," added Carrie.

"My mother!" called out a young handsome dark-haired youth.

Everyone laughed.

"There's so much information out there," Pamela warned, "You have to narrow down the information and get what's most effective. A critical skill we need today is to be able select the best information and avoid the rest."

"So it's good to read books by well-known people in your field?" said Glenn.

"That's it exactly," agreed Pamela.

2. Model the Best People

"I know what that means," said Cindy warming to the topic. "If Glenn wants to be a great chef he needs to find a great chef he'd like to emulate."

"Ooh, emulate," teased Glenn.

CHAPTER ONE: CHANGING YOUR MINDSET

3. Examine Your Current Beliefs

"I know what that one means," said Carrie. "If I want to be a writer, I should look at what I believe. I should make sure my mindset fits my aspirations. Maybe my beliefs are limiting my desire to be a writer."

"Ooh, aspirations!" Glenn teased. "I'm bringing a dictionary to the next session!"

4. Shape Your Mindset with Vision and Goals

"Can anyone explain this one?" asked Pamela as she moved to the next slide.

"I'll take a stab at it," volunteered the middle-aged man with the toupee. "If you have a clear vision of what you want to do and have mapped out a plan for getting there, then that shapes your mindset."

"Exactly right, Ian!" exclaimed Pamela.

5. Find Your Voice

"This one is my favorite," said Pamela moving to the next slide. I want all of you to read Stephen Covey's book, The 8th Habit before we meet next week. In it he talks about finding your voice."

"Is there a movie version?" Glenn asked.

Cindy snorted.

"Not exactly Glenn," replied Pamela. "But you can get an audio version."

"Never mind," said Glenn. "I'll just go to her house and she'll read it to me!"

"Deal," said Cindy high-fiving him, "But you have to cook me dinner!"

"You're on!" agreed Glenn.

Pamela flashed the last slide and paused while everyone read:

> **1. What are you good at? That's your mind.**
>
> **2. What do you love doing? That's your heart.**
>
> **3. What need can you fill? That's the body.**
>
> **4. What is life asking of you? What gives your life meaning and purpose? What do you feel like you should be doing? What is your conscience directing you to do? That is your spirit.**

"Your voice is what you express authentically. It is the unique gift that you can add to the world!" said Pamela. "I look forward to hearing the unique gift each of you can add to the world, next week. Avoid those who think you cannot do what you truly believe you can and want to do! See you next week everyone."

"Well, what did you think?" asked Glenn.

"Surprisingly interesting," admitted Cindy.

CHAPTER ONE: CHANGING YOUR MINDSET

"So, what night's good for you and what would you like me to cook?"

"Saturday. Be there early. It's a long book!" Cindy said.

SWEET LEMONADE

TAKE A SIP

Discovering Your Unique Gift

**Question #1:
What are you good at?**

_____
_____
_____
_____

**Question #2:
What do you love doing?**

_____
_____
_____
_____

**Question #3:
What need can you fill?**

_____
_____
_____
_____

CHAPTER ONE: CHANGING YOUR MINDSET

Question #4:
What is life asking of you?
_____
_____
_____
_____

Question #5:
What gives your life meaning and purpose?
_____
_____
_____
_____

Question #6:
What do you feel like you should be doing?
_____
_____
_____
_____

Question #7:
What is your conscious directing you to do?
_____
_____
_____
_____

Notes:

Chapter Two:
Fulfilling Purpose

Never surrender your hopes and dreams to the fateful limitations others have placed on their own lives. The vision of your true destiny does not reside within the blinkered outlook of the naysayers and the doom prophets. Judge not by their words, but accept advice based on the evidence of actual results.
~Anton St. Maarten

Little by little, Cindy was finding her mindset. The twelve sessions had helped her explore who she was and what she was good at. That one was pretty tough as she was convinced she was good at nothing.

"What do you love doing?" Glenn asked her one night, in frustration. "You're good at lots of things. You're smart. You're witty. You're a good listener. You can do anything you set out to do. What need can you fill?"

"Well," said Cindy hesitantly, "I love to work with animals."

"There you have it, then," said Andrew. "Your purpose is working with animals."

"Veterinary college is way expensive and I'd never get in," protested Cindy. "You need documented time spent working with animals before they will even look at your application. How can I convince a college board to pick me when I wouldn't even pick me?"

When Clarisse heard Cindy's decision she immediately approved. "Even as a…um…challenging teen," she said, "Marmalade always liked and trusted you."

"That fat, old, yellow cat?" asked Cindy. "That's because I used to sneak her snacks!"

"Nevertheless," said Clarisse, refusing to be sidetracked, "Marmalade was an excellent judge of character."

"Yes, well, unfortunately Marmalade is not on the college admissions board and cannot document my time spent helping her retain her fat cat status."

"Well, that may be but Marmalade's veterinarian just happens to be on that board," Clarisse commented.

"No sh%@?" Cindy sputtered.

"Language, Cindy," Clarisse commented.

CHAPTER TWO: FULFILLING PURPOSE

"Sorry," said Cindy. "Old habits. How is Marmalade's vet going to be any help? She doesn't even know me."

"Ah, but she knows me," Clarisse responded. "You don't have a cat for twenty-three years without building a friendship with her veterinarian."

"Holy crap!" exclaimed Cindy. "Marmalade was twenty-three?"

"Yes indeed. Thanks to excellent health care and a pampered lifestyle."

"But there's still the matter of documented volunteer time."

"I was just getting to that," replied Clarisse. "Dr. Glover has a volunteer program and I am sure she can find a spot for you. It won't be glamorous but it will give you volunteer animal experience…and help you decide for sure that this is your purpose."

"Why are you doing this, Clarisse?" asked Cindy.

"Well, Cindy, I watched you grow up," said Clarisse.

"More like screw up," muttered Cindy.

"Well, there is that, yes," Clarisse admitted, chuckling. "But you always came back better off for the experience."

"And yet to screw up again," mumbled Cindy.

"Don't be so hard on yourself, dear," said Clarisse. "We all made our mistakes."

"I'll bet you didn't!" said Cindy.

"Well perhaps I wasn't quite as—err—creative as you were," conceded Clarisse. "But, I had my moments. And, I always believed that, with a hand up, you'd eventually find your life's purpose."

"You never gave up on me," said Cindy. "Why did you bother?"

"Let's just say that is part of my life's purpose to help you fulfill yours."

"I don't understand," said Cindy. "How will I know if this is my purpose? What's a purpose anyhow?"

"I can answer that," said a pleasant male voice.

"Good evening, Pastor Mike," said Clarisse, giving the tall gray-haired man in the black suit a hug.

"Hello, Clarisse," Pastor Mike greeted the tall elderly woman affectionately. Then turning, he took both of Cindy's hands in his and said warmly, "And you must be Cindy. I am so happy to meet you!"

"You too, Pastor Mike. Clarisse talks about you all the time. I think she was hoping I'd see the light."

"All in God's time, Cindy," replied Pastor Mike. His brown eyes twinkled. "You were asking about life's purpose when I came in."

CHAPTER TWO: FULFILLING PURPOSE

"Yes, Pastor," said Cindy. "How do you know what your purpose is?"

"That's a very good question, Cindy. You see, we were all created by God for a special purpose and destiny. And when you have found that purpose, you will feel truly fulfilled."

"They broke the mold on guardian angels when they made Clarisse," said Cindy.

"Oh, please," said Clarisse. "I'm far from an angel—although I do appreciate the compliment. You might start by asking yourself: What makes me smile? That might be people, events, activities, or hobbies. Then ask yourself: What are my favorite things to do?"

"Those are good questions, Clarisse," said Pastor Mike. "Here's another one: What makes you feel great about yourself?"

"Cindy and I talked about what she is naturally good at," commented Clarisse.

"A good way to measure that," said Pastor Mike, "is to ask yourself: What do people typically ask me for my help?"

Clarisse added, "I always ask myself: Given my talents, passions, and values, how can I use these to serve my fellow human, to help others in need, to contribute to my community?

"Wow!" exclaimed Cindy, "those are Mother Teresa questions."

"Another strategy you might try is to write out a personal mission statement. This gives you a clear sense of purpose. It describes who you are and how you will live. It forces you to think through your priorities carefully, and make your actions fit those priorities."

"Wow!" said Cindy. "I have no idea how to do that."

Just ask yourself: What do I want to do? Who can help me? What do I hope will be the outcome?"

"Thanks Pastor Mike," said Cindy. "I think I can do that."

"You're welcome, Cindy," said Pastor Mike. "If you ever need anything—just to talk, you know where I hang out."

"Yes Pastor Mike. Clarisse has pointed that out to me on several occasions!"

"Well, you two, it's time for dinner," said Clarisse. "My purpose is to make sure everyone is fed. Come along!"

"Does everyone find their purpose?" asked Cindy.

"Oh, sadly, no," said Pastor Mike. A shadow crossed his handsome features. "Many people are lost. They are really searching for their purpose but they don't know it. They just feel that there is something missing in their lives."

"How do they know they even have a purpose? How do any of us know?"

CHAPTER TWO: FULFILLING PURPOSE

"I believe your purpose lives inside you," explained Pastor Mike. "Life is a journey. As you live it, you become aware of who you are, and what your purpose is. Every person was placed on earth to live a rich and purposeful life."

"So how do you find out what that purpose it?" asked Cindy. "Not everyone is lucky enough to have a pushy, in-your-face neighbor like Clarisse."

"You're right," agreed Pastor Mike, laughing. "But if we look around, there is someone who will help us find our way. We just have to be receptive to that help."

"Well, I have to admit, I wasn't always receptive to Clarisse's help. Man! I hated her when she ratted me out to my parents. I used to think she was an old busybody."

"I am an old busybody!" Clarisse said proudly. "While you were doing the devil's business I was out doing God's work."

"Yes, you were, Clarisse," admitted Cindy. "Even when I resented the h—heck out of you for it, I knew I was wrong."

"And I knew you would eventually see the light," said Clarisse. "Pass the potato salad please."

Pastor Mike rose from the table and glanced at his watch. "Thanks for a delicious dinner, Clarisse. I must be on my way. Men's prayer group tonight. Cindy it was a pleasure. You just keep following your guardian angel, here. It's important to have a coach. Remember. I'm here if you need me. I'm pretty easy to find."

"Good-bye Pastor Mike and thanks again for helping me out on that purpose question."

"You're welcome, Cindy. Just remember: You don't have to deal with life's challenges alone. Every successful person has a coach. Think of every successful person has a coach to help, support, and directs them toward their purpose."

Even super stars like Einstein knew how important coaches were," agreed Clarisse. "He said, 'It takes a different kind of thinking to solve a problem than the kind of thinking which produced the problem.' Coaching is merely helping people develop their thinking about their problems, relationships, careers, and their future in creative ways. A coach or mentor or advisor—or even a fairy godmother if you will—helps you clarify your purpose. Your coach supports you through your fears. She keeps you focused, and helps you change your limiting beliefs. Your coach helps you develop strategies to move your toward accomplishing your purpose."

"You've known all along where I needed to go and what I needed to do, haven't you Clarisse?" asked Cindy in awe.

"I was optimistic, Cindy," said Clarisse.

"But why bother? You have to admit I wasn't very receptive."

"Oh, I love a good challenge," said Clarisse, laughing. "God sends us only the trials He knows we can handle."

"But I wasn't your problem," persisted Cindy. "And I wasn't very appreciative."

CHAPTER TWO: FULFILLING PURPOSE

"I was serious when I said this was my purpose," admitted Clarisse. "And someone was my mentor. So I am merely paying it forward. Someday you will too."

"Thanks, Clarisse," said Cindy, hugging the tall, elderly woman.

"Now, how about some dessert?" asked Clarisse.

SWEET LEMONADE

TAKE A SIP

Your Life Purpose

Write 3 ways you can be supported in fulfilling your life purpose:

_____
_____
_____
_____
_____
_____
_____
_____
_____
_____
_____
_____
_____
_____
_____
_____
_____
_____
_____

CHAPTER TWO: FULFILLING PURPOSE

Notes:

Chapter Three:
Spirituality

Life isn't about finding yourself, it's about discovering who God created you to be.
~Unknown

"Clarisse, what are you doing today?" asked Cindy one morning. "I need your help with something."

"I can always push weeding those flower beds off for another day," replied Clarisse. "What's on your mind?"

"I'd like to go and talk to Pastor Mike about becoming a Christian and I'd really like you to go with me."

"I'd be delighted to do that, Cindy. Let me see if Pastor Mike has time to talk to us today. I'll invite him for dinner. The poor man can't boil water and his housekeeper is an immaculate cleaner but she's no cook." Clarisse was already dialing the church office.

"Pastor Mike? Can you come for dinner?" asked Clarisse. "Cindy would like to talk to you."

"Wow! You move fast," exclaimed Cindy.

"He'll be here at six," replied Clarisse.

"Why do I think I am all part of a plan?" Cindy asked.

"We're all part of God's plan," Clarisse said. "Now what shall we serve for dinner?"

True to his word, Pastor Mike rang Clarisse's bell at six on the dot. "I brought dessert," he announced when Clarisse opened the door.

When they had eaten a delicious dinner and consumed Pastor Mike's dessert, Cindy broached the reason for her asking to meet with Pastor Mike. "As you know, Pastor Mike, my parents are not church goers so I have a lot of questions and doubts. I've made a lot of mistakes in my life and I am not sure why God—or anyone else—would want to be bothered with me. But you and Clarisse seem to have such joy and purpose in your lives. Frankly, that inspires me to explore Christianity."

"First of all you don't have to be a Christian to believe in God but you do need your fellow Christians to support you on your quest to find your place in the world. You need their support in the tough times. And there will be tough times. I like to tell people seeking to find their way what Hans Urs von Balthasar says in his book, Prayer, 'What you are is God's gift to you, what you become is your gift to God.'"

CHAPTER THREE: SPIRITUALITY

"Of course God wants to be bothered with you, Cindy," said Clarisse. "After all, you are His creation."

"I have a lot of doubts, Pastor Mike. I envy you and Clarisse the strength of your faith."

"We didn't always have this faith, Cindy," Pastor Mike pointed out. Everyone accepts Christ in a different way and at different times. Sometimes, it's like a bolt of lightning—a complete epiphany. Others accept Him gradually, little by little."

"As a great writer Osho pointed out, 'You will have to create the path by walking yourself; the path is not ready-made, lying there and waiting for you. It is just like the sky: the birds fly, but they don't leave any footprints. You cannot follow them; there are no footprints left behind.'" Clarisse said.

"Clarisse is right," Pastor Mike said. "But we can read the Bible and learn about how we are to walk and live as Christians and that provides us with the guidance we need."

"But how will I know when I've found Christianity?" Cindy asked.

"Remember when we discussed how to find your purpose in life?" asked Pastor Mike.

Cindy nodded.

"Well, some people seem to find their life purpose easier than others. God really does have a plan for every single person. It's just that it takes some of us longer to see what that purpose is."

"Did you always want to be a pastor?" asked Cindy.

"Oh my goodness, no!" said Pastor Mike, laughing. "In my teens I wanted to be a rock star!"

"You did?" asked Cindy in amazement. "What made you change your mind?"

"My friends in the band went off to college to become doctors and lawyers. That left me a solo performer and, quite frankly it was scary and lonely without them. So, I struggled with what to do with my life. The person I admired most was Pastor Frank. As we talked about what I did that made me happy and how I felt I could best make a contribution to the world, it suddenly occurred to me that I wanted to do what Pastor Frank was doing. I guess you could call it an epiphany moment."

"Have you ever felt you made the wrong decision?" asked Cindy.

"Not even for a moment," said Pastor Mike confidently. "This is my life's purpose."

"Okay," said Cindy. I get that finding your life purpose means doing something you are good at and you truly love. What if things aren't so clear? What if you're not sure what you are good at and what you love to do? What if you haven't discovered any special talent? What if that talent turns out to be not such a good thing after all? What if you were wrong?"

"Don't panic," soothed Pastor Mike. "There are lots of people who feel like that. Look at Jesus' disciples. They were

CHAPTER THREE: SPIRITUALITY

fishermen, tax collectors, and farmers. They were probably good at what they did. They were making a living at it for their families," observed Pastor Mike.

"But Jesus showed them their truth. Following God became their new purpose," noted Clarisse. "We don't always start out knowing our purpose. I believed I was meant to teach. Then, along came my husband and three babies and I realized God had a different purpose for my life. My new purpose made me happy and fulfilled just like the disciples new purpose did for them."

"What we're saying, Cindy," said Pastor Mike, "don't over complicate things and don't be afraid to try something you feel you're good at and something you love. If it isn't God's purpose for you, He will show you the way."

"Where do I start?" asked Cindy.

"Right here," replied Pastor Mike, holding up a Bible. "All you have to do is read this," said Pastor Mike. "The answers are in here."

"But what does being a Christian mean?" asked Cindy. "Does it mean giving big bunches of money to the church and going to mass every Sunday? Frankly, I've watched some of those people being not very pleasant the rest of the week."

"You're right, Cindy," said Clarice. "Being nice to others—even when you don't feel like it, or they don't deserve it is all part of being a Christian."

"Forgiving people, and loving those who aren't very lovable, is also part of being a Christian," said Pastor Mike.

"Clarisse taught me that!" commented Cindy. "I wasn't very lovable."

Clarisse laughed and hugged Cindy. "You were always lovable, Cindy. Sometimes you weren't very likable."

"So, let me get this straight," said Cindy. "This Christian stuff is linked to what I am going to do with myself when I grow up because my life purpose is all part of God's plan. And when I—if I—become a Christian, it will be easier to discover what God has in store for me?"

"When you begin to grow as a Christian, He is able to work through you. You'll discover your purpose in life. Getting really good at being a Christian means you focus on others and not on yourself. You look for ways to reach out to others who need your help," explained Pastor Mike.

"Like you and Clarisse are always thinking of someone else," commented Cindy.

"We try to do that," agreed Clarisse. "There's a payback for us too. When your focus is on helping others who need it, we receive direction in our own lives."

"When you focus on another's need, God focuses on your needs," Pastor Mike explained.

"When you work with God to find your life purpose, you're part of a team," Clarisse noted.

"Try something you're good at," encouraged Pastor Mike. "If it isn't the right fit, you'll find out—no harm done."

CHAPTER THREE: SPIRITUALITY

"It takes time, Cindy," warned Clarisse. "You must be patient. God isn't going to show you everything all at once."

"No one has the answers about what's right for you. The decision is yours. Trust your intuition and listen to God," advised Pastor Mike.

"And don't give up if you don't immediately get a message from God. It happens on His time—not yours," cautioned Clarisse.

"I've brought you some reading," said Pastor Mike handing Cindy a box.

Cindy withdrew several books and laid them out beside the Bible Pastor Mike had given her earlier.

- The Shack by Wm. Paul Young
- Simply Christian by N. T. Wright
- Making Good Habits by Joyce Meyer
- The God You Can Know by Dan DeHaan
- Knowing God by J. Packer
- The Truth of the Cross by R. C. Sproule
- Mere Christianity by C. S. Lewis
- The Purpose Driven Life by Rick Warren
- Christ Our Mediator by C.J. Mahaney

"Well, it looks as if I have my work cut out for me," said Cindy.

"Take your time, Cindy," said Pastor Mike. "And if you ever need to talk, you know where to find me."

"Thanks, Pastor Mike," said Cindy. "Would you mind if, while I am reading these, I come to your services?"

"You're always welcome!"

"I'll pick you up at eight," said Clarisse.

"Why does that not surprise me?" asked Cindy, laughing.

CHAPTER THREE: SPIRITUALITY

TAKE A SIP

Spiritual Growth

What 3 books can you read that will inspire you?

1.

2.

3.

SWEET LEMONADE

Notes:

Chapter Four:
Good Parenting

When you are getting ready to become a mom, being in love with someone just isn't enough. You need to think about whether he would be a good parent and raise your children with similar beliefs.
~Cindy Crawford

"You and Derek seem to be hitting it off," commented Clarisse one pleasant summer day over lunch in her backyard.

"Derek is a really nice guy but I am not sure we are cut out to be together," Cindy commented.

"Why?" asked Clarisse. "You certainly seem happy to be together. It's so nice to see him smile. It's been a rough three years for him."

"I know," agreed Cindy. "But that's part of the problem. I'm don't think I have what it takes to be a parent and there are two little girls who desperately need a mother."

"Don't you like the girls?" asked Clarisse.

"Oh, I love those little girls. But, I'm not sure I'm what they need in their lives."

"Why would you think that?" asked Clarisse, looking puzzled.

"Well my first try at parenting was a dismal failure as you well know."

"I'd hardly call that a failure, Cindy. You were sixteen with your future ahead of you and no resources nor a supportive partner to think about keeping that baby. Giving him up for adoption to that couple who so badly wanted a baby was the most precious gift you could have given that baby."

"But that's my only experience at being a good parent. How do I know if I can be a good parent?"

"You're a good and loving person, Cindy. If you want this, you'll make Derek and those two little girls the center of your universe."

"But what am I getting myself into?"

"I've got a great idea!" exclaimed Clarisse.

"Why does that not surprise me?" joked Cindy.

"I volunteer at the Early Years Centre every Wednesday. I hold an effective parenting workshop for parents who are struggling. Why don't you come along with me and we'll pose your question to the participants?"

CHAPTER FOUR: GOOD PARENTING

"Do you think they'd mind?" asked Cindy.

"They are all there to learn how to cope as parents. I think they'd find discussing your question very useful."

"Okay then. Thanks, Clarisse."

"I'll pick you up at seven," said Clarisse.

"Does this seem familiar?" asked Cindy.

They both laughed.

༺༻

"Good evening everyone, Clarisse greeted the eight people assembled in the meeting hall of a church. I've brought a friend with me. She's struggling with parenting issues. She's got a lot of concerns. I suggested she share them with you. Together I hope we can come up with some answers that will help all of us. This is Cindy."

"Hello, everybody," Cindy said. "Thanks for letting me be a part of your group today. I really need some help."

"So what kind of questions do you have and why would you think loser parents like us could help?" said a frowning woman with spiky red hair. She appeared to be in her mid-thirties. Clearly she had a chip on her shoulder.

"Gina, remember what I said," reminded Clarisse quietly. "If you were loser parents you wouldn't be here trying to improve the quality of your parenting skills."

"Yeah? Tell that to my teenage son!" Gina shot back. "He thinks I can't do anything right."

"Wait until he's twenty-one," a pretty blonde in her mid-forties replied. "I became brilliant when Neil turned twenty-one and needed me to sign his loan for a start-up business."

"Thanks for sharing that, Janet," said Clarisse. "We do indeed look a lot smarter to our kids once they get a little older and farther from those teen hormones! You hang in there Gina. Janet's right. But Cindy's situation is a little different. Tell them Cindy."

"Well," Cindy started, "I've been seeing a great guy who has two young daughters."

"Oh, oh," said a dark-haired twenty-something woman. "Step children. Look out. You'll always be the wicked stepmother, the woman who destroyed their dad's life."

"Oh, it's not like that," Cindy protested.

"Cindy's situation is different from yours, Jennifer," Clarice added. "The girls' mom died of cancer when they were two and four."

"My problem is: How do I know if I can be a good parent?" asked Cindy.

"Do you love these girls?" asked Sam, a striking African American in her late twenties."

CHAPTER FOUR: GOOD PARENTING

"Oh yes!" Cindy said without hesitation. "I just am not sure I have what it takes to be a good parent."

"Let's share with Cindy some of the things we've learned in the group," suggested Clarisse. "Sam why don't you start?"

"Rule number one," Sam said seriously. "Never let your kids get bigger than you are!"

Everyone in the group laughed.

"Seriously," said Sam. "Sometimes the best thing you can give your children is love and affection. A warm touch or a big hug lets your kids know you care about them. They're never too old to hug and kiss—even though they will protest if anyone is looking."

"Hugs and kisses aren't the only way to show affection," added Jennifer. "My kids respond to a pat on the back, a handshake, a high five or even a 'Well done!'"

"The hardest thing for me to get through to my kids was that I still loved them no matter how angry they made me."

"Kids need to experience lots of hugs and kisses right from the time they are born," said Janet. "I wish my parents had done that. It would have been easier for me to understand how important this is for all kids if I'd had better role models for parenting."

Catherine, a small brunette spoke up for the first time. "Your kids thrive on praise," she said. "Praise is one of the most important parts of being a good parent. When

I brought that awful kindergarten finger painting home from school, my mother—who is an artist—used to rave about how talented I was. She framed my work and hung it in her art studio. One day, a customer, thinking my work was a new abstract, tried to buy one of my paintings. My mom said everything in the studio was for sale except those paintings. They were priceless to her. She gave me the confidence to go out and try to make a career as an artist. I miss her."

Gina said, "My mom always told my pop you should praise a child at least three times as often as you criticized her. That was hard for pops. He was raised in an Italian household where parents were physical with hugs and kisses but also slaps. He saw no need for praising. He thought it was his job to keep us on the straight and narrow."

"I think every child should be cherished for their own merits," added Sam. "My twin sister was the perfect child—great student, beautiful girl, athletic, a good writer. I always walked in her shadow until I discovered music. Sarah couldn't carry a tune and her fingers got all tied up on the piano keys. My parents made a huge fuss over my musical ability. They even bought me a set of drums and let my band practice in the basement. They never compared the two of us—just celebrated the things each of us did well. I hope I can be as good a parent to the twins as they were."

Catherine said, "I know you're going to laugh when I say this because I don't usually talk but communication is important. You need to be able to talk and listen to your kids. My mother was an actress. When she wasn't on stage she played the role of mother. She talked at us kids. She never

CHAPTER FOUR: GOOD PARENTING

stopped to ask us anything and she never listened to us. I vowed I'd listen and react to everything my kids said."

"That's one thing I do right," commented Jennifer. "I set aside a time to talk to my daughter every day. Just before bedtime I ask her to tell me one funny thing, one thing she learned and one thing she wished had happened differently. When she says she has to tell me something, I drop what I'm doing and give her my full attention,"

"I have four children," Gina said. "I try to spend time with each one. I divide my time so each one of them gets equal alone time with me. We go to the park or the museum or the library or just spend time in the backyard together. When I have each of them alone I find out stuff like what they want to be, things they like to do and what they are worried about."

"Never miss the big events," added Sam. "My husband was a big important company man who gave us a fancy home and a big car and lots of things. But he was never around for the birthday parties, the graduations, the school plays and that winning soccer goal. The kids resented it and I think he realizes today what he missed."

"Maybe it's my Italian Catholic background talking here," said Gina. "But I believe children need something to believe in. They need a base to carry them through the tough times. My church has carried many a lost soul through trying times. Family is important but they need a Higher Power to turn to."

"I agree, Gina," said Cindy. "After a lot of reading and soul searching, I've recently become a Christian. It has made me feel so different about myself and my future."

"Well, our time is up for tonight," announced Clarisse. "Thanks for sharing your thoughts with Cindy."

"I have learned a lot tonight, everyone. I think you are wonderful people—and great parents. I see that how you feel about your kids is important. It also seems to me that many of you have learned good parenting strategies by listening to your kids."

"Kids don't come with an owner's manual," quipped Sam. "Like gardening, you've got to get in there and dig. Groups like this give us a place to vent and a sympathetic ear."

"I'd like to come back when I become a parent to Derek's two little girls," said Cindy.

"You'd better!" said Janet. "You made Cathy talk!"

TAKE A SIP

Parenting children involves discretion. There is no one standard rule for all children. Good parenting helps foster honesty, self-control, kindness, empathy, caring, sharing, and loving.

SWEET LEMONADE

Notes:

Chapter Five:
Act like a Lady

Your dresses should be tight enough to show you're a woman and loose enough to show you're a lady.
~Edith Head

"What are you reading?" asked Clarisse as she looked over the fence that separated her yard from Cindy's.

"*Miss Manners' Etiquette for Young Ladies*," said Cindy holding up the book.

"Whatever for?" asked Clarisse.

"Derek's parents are coming to town and they're taking us to the Country Club for dinner. You know he comes from a very posh family and I am petrified I'll make a fool of myself," Cindy admitted, sighing. "But this book isn't much help."

"What's the problem?" asked Clarisse.

"Listen to this," Cindy said. "'Just as manners, and attitudes have evolved over time, so too has the idea of what it means to be a *lady*.'"

"Oh, I see," said Clarisse.

"There's more," said Cindy, reading on. "'Though the term lady may sound passé, certain ladylike behaviors remain constant. These include: elegance, courtesy, and respect for self and others.'"

"Well, that seems logical," remarked Clarisse.

"It may be logical," said Cindy. "But I have no idea how it translates to how I can act like a lady."

"I have an idea!" said Clarisse jubilantly. "My friend Lady Jane Powell—yes Lady Jane—used to run an etiquette school for young ladies of the south. I'm sure I can get her to come visit for tea this afternoon."

"Why am I not surprised that you just happen to know the perfect person to offer advice, Clarisse?" responded Cindy. "Your network of useful people is endless."

"It's all about having the right connections," Clarisse said humbly, blushing at the compliment.

"Thanks, again, Clarisse," said Cindy. "Sometime I look forward to being able to do something for you."

CHAPTER FIVE: ACT LIKE A LADY

"I'll go and call her right away. Hmmm. I am thinking cucumber and watercress sandwiches and those mini éclair," she said to herself as she went inside to call her friend.

༄

At precisely three that afternoon, Clarisse's doorbell rang. There stood a very nervous Cindy. She was wearing a slim green cocktail dress and strappy shoes. In one sweaty hand she clutched a glittery silver bag.

"Well, don't you clean up nicely," Clarisse deadpanned.

"I hope so," remarked Cindy. "It took me two hours. I am so nervous!"

"Come in. Lady Jane will be along soon. May I offer you something to drink?"

"Oh, I'd love one but I am so edgy I'd probably spill it."

"We can get started by rehearsing introductions," suggested Clarisse. "Since I am talking with you now, when Lady Jane appears, I will say, '"Cindy, I'd like to introduce my friend, Lady Jane Powell.' Then I'll add a thoughtful detail about Lady Jane such as "'I know you will find Lady Jane's tips on etiquette useful. Lady Jane and I have been friends since finishing school.'"

"I didn't know you went to finishing school, Clarisse," Cindy said.

"And so will you today," Clarisse remarked. "Where I come from finishing school is almost mandatory—along with ballroom dancing and learning how to cross stitch."

Just then the bell rang. "Show time!" called Clarisse cheerily. Cindy groaned. A well-dressed slim brunette woman entered the living room with Clarisse.

"Lady Jane may I present my dear friend, Cindy. We've been next door neighbors since Cindy was born," said Clarisse.

"It is so nice to meet you Lady Jane. Clarisse speaks glowingly of your finishing school days. Thank you for coming. I appreciate your willingness to share your expertise," said Cindy shaking hands with Lady Jane.

"Oh Clarisse," said Lady Jane. "She's perfectly delightful! I am pleased to make your acquaintance, Cindy. Clarisse has a special fondness for you. Please call me Jane."

"Thank you," answered Cindy.

"Shall we have tea and talk?" suggested Clarisse.

"What a lovely idea," answered Lady Jane. "I have been looking forward to high tea all day. It's a lost art in this country, you know."

As they dined elegantly on tiny watercress and cucumber sandwiches, tea and petit fours, Lady Jane asked Cindy, "Why the hysteria over etiquette, Cindy?"

CHAPTER FIVE: ACT LIKE A LADY

"My fiancé's mother is coming to the city to meet me and take us out to the country club for dinner. I am petrified of making a blunder. His mother is an aristocrat."

"My first lesson is one you already know and many so-called aristocrats fail to do. Always say please and thank you whether you are addressing a peer, someone you hired, or a tradesperson. Failure to do so is just plain rude. I hear your good manners and I sense you use them no matter who you are addressing."

"I believe I do that."

"Extend this thanks to written notes for gifts, favors…In your written notes add details of the gift or favor so it isn't a pat thanks. It's personalized."

"My mom did a good job of teaching me to write thank you notes."

"This next one rarely makes the pages of any etiquette book but I believe it is the sign of a real lady. It's being able to say no politely yet emphatically."

"I'm not sure how that fits in, Jane," said Clarisse.

"It's simple, my friend," commented Lady Jane. "A lady frequently has to say no to a dance, a date, dinner, alcohol, or a fattening dessert—not to mention volunteering for a charity for which she just does not have the time."

"I get it," said Cindy. "It's all part of being your own person and standing up for yourself—but doing so with finesse."

"Absolutely right, Cindy," said Lady Jane. "Don't let others pressure you into doing what you know is just not right for you."

"That's good advice, Jane," commented Clarisse.

"Never stop learning, Cindy," added Lady Jane. "There are those who will say you are putting on airs or aiming above your station. Don't listen to them. A lady is well read. She can converse intelligently. She knows about current world events. That doesn't mean she tells everything she knows to impress others. It means she can join a conversation knowledgeably. A lady is also a good listener. She makes others think she values what they have to say."

"How do you stay current, Lady Jane?" asked Cindy.

"Oh I read and watch documentaries," commented Lady Jane. "Thanks to the Internet no one has an excuse to be uninformed about what's going on around her. Good scholarly articles on every topic imaginable are available at the click of a mouse. There are also lots of options at the local library and the nearest college campus."

"Wow. I never considered all those possibilities," commented Cindy.

"Let's look into some of them tomorrow," suggested Clarisse. "What else do you have for us, Jane?" she inquired.

"This may seem picky and outdated but body language says so much about a person. I am a stickler for good posture in my students," said Jane. "Let me explain. Standing and sitting up straight are signs of a true lady. Plus your clothes look better on you! It requires some training at first but it will become automatic."

"I've always admired Clarisse's posture," admitted Cindy.

"Ah the old book-on-the-head for an hour a night!" Clarisse commented drily. "Miss Armstrong would be pleased."

"My next point is common sense, common courtesy and often overlooked by those impressed with their own importance. You see: Being a lady isn't just about looking or behaving properly on the outside. More importantly, it involves being a good person on the inside. In this day of tablets and smart phones and texting and talking this is becoming a tougher and tougher one. But it is important. Show your respect for others. When talking to someone, give that person your undivided attention. Don't interrupt or talk over others."

"Many of your excellent suggestions are about being a good person not just a lady, aren't they, Jane?" commented Clarisse.

"Indeed they are," agreed Jane. "Being a good person is going to put you well along the road to being a lady. For example: Help to those in need. It could mean helping an elderly person carry groceries, or volunteering at a homeless shelter, a food bank, or animal shelter."

"Cindy is doing volunteer work for Marmalade's veterinarian," commented Clarisse.

"My heavens!" exclaimed Jane. "Is that old mop still alive?"

"No," responded Clarisse. "Sadly dear Marmalade has passed on. But her veterinarian and I have remained good friends."

"And why not?" said Jane. "Marmalade's maladies built that clinic."

"I feel that Marmalade would approve of Cindy's project. I think she is smiling down at Cindy,"

"Only if Cindy brought treats," snorted Lady Jane.

Cindy giggled.

"But I digress," said Lady Jane. "Ladies are always charming."

"Seriously," said Cindy, "short of charm school, how does one do that?"

"Well," said Clarisse, "for starters, if you don't know how to be charming, smile more at people. Talk to them. Compliment them more—but genuinely."

"A lady is careful in all she says," added Clarisse.

"And in how she says it," commented Lady Jane. She fixed Cindy with a knowing look.

"Well, yes," Cindy murmured. "That's a work in progress."

"A lady never uses profanity nor gets drunk and abusive. You see: Being a lady is about exercising self-control. Swearing and over-imbibing are example of overindulgence."

CHAPTER FIVE: ACT LIKE A LADY

"Got it," agreed Cindy.

"I can tell a lot about a woman by the way her children behave when they come to my house," Lady Jane said.

"How so?" asked Cindy.

"Well, a lady is respectful of others' property. When you are a guest in somebody else's home, you should wait for the host or hostess to ask you to be seated and to give you direction about where to leave your purse and your coat and whether to remove your shoes. Children who are well brought up do this."

"I never thought about this but you are absolutely right. That's true too about holding doors open for people and offering to help someone who may be experiencing difficulty," noted Clarisse. "When I had my crutches the best brought up children always reached for the door or offered to help, without any prodding from parents."

"My last bit of advice is be like a duck."

"A duck?" asked Cindy.

"Yes," explained Lady Jane. "On the surface appear calm and unflappable. Never let them see you sweat. Under the surface you may be paddling like heck. They don't know that! Don't lash out at others if you are annoyed, angry, or upset. Remain cool and poised. Handle the situation like a pro: rationally and calmly. Never do or say things in the heat of the moment that you will regret later. You can't unring a bell and you can't unsay the words."

"Lady Jane, thank you so much," said Cindy. "You've given me a lot to think about but surprisingly I feel more prepared to meet Derek's mother."

"I am sure you will get along swimmingly!" said Lady Jane.

"Let's meet again after Cindy's dinner," suggested Clarisse. "We can debrief over asparagus and asiago quiche."

"I'd travel across the country for your cooking, Clarisse," said Lady Jane. "Thank you again for the delightful tea."

"Good-bye Jane," said Clarisse.

"Well milady," said Clarisse turning toward Cindy, "Real ladies know how to do dishes!"

"Yes we do!" said Cindy, hugging Clarisse.

"And real ladies don't mind getting their hands wet," chortled Clarisse.

"And real ladies don't find kitchen duties beneath them," added Cindy.

"I'll bet Derek's mother doesn't do dishes," Clarisse observed.

"I'll bet you're right," agreed Cindy. "But her son knows how to do them."

"Ah, a Renaissance man!" said Clarisse.

"Indeed," said Cindy. "He knows how to do laundry too."

CHAPTER FIVE: ACT LIKE A LADY

"Is he different from other men you've had in your life?" asked Clarisse.

"Oh, Clarisse!" Cindy sighed. "That is definitely a story for another day!"

SWEET LEMONADE

TAKE A SIP

Ladies:
Showing a great amount of skin when you dress up isn't the way to find prince charming. Prince charming likes his gifts wrapped.

CHAPTER FIVE: ACT LIKE A LADY

NOTES:

Chapter Six:
The Man

*Men always want to be a woman's first love -
women like to be a man's last romance*
~Oscar Wilde

"Listen to this," said Clarisse, reading from the local paper, "If you want your partner to treat you with dignity, you need to demand that."

"Nice theory on paper, isn't it?" Cindy commented. "Mostly your demands will get him walking out the door."

"We've all been there," said Clarisse.

"Not you!" scoffed Cindy. "I've never met anyone who is so confident and comfortable in herself."

"Age changes a lot of things," Clarisse commented. "Like the girl in the advice column I was guilty of doing all sorts of things to please the boyfriend of the day."

Cindy laughed. "Isn't it amazing the trouble we'd go to be appealing to the males around us? I used to get up two hours early so my hair was just right before I left for school and if it wasn't going just right, I'd have a meltdown. I'll bet no boy even looked at my hair."

"I slept on those huge rollers with the brushes in them so my hair would be just the right amount of curls without being frizzy."

"Ouch!" exclaimed Cindy. "My girlfriend had curly hair and she used to get her mom to flat iron it every morning. One day the flat iron was a little hot and it singed the hair. A piece actually fell out."

"I was a teenager during the era of the beehive. We'd back-comb the heck out of our hair, then spray it and make this mile high hairdo. We thought we were so cool."

"I wonder what today's crop of teenage girls do to stand out?"

"Spend a few hours in the mall and you'll find out," responded Cindy. "Iridescent colors, and extensions are big."

"So the price of awesome hair has gone up," Cindy observed.

"Exactly," Clarisse agreed. "Kids do what we did. They emulate their favorite movie stars and sports heroes."

"Ah, yes," recalled Cindy. "I'd forgotten about the Dorothy Hamill wedge.

"Now it's the Mylie Cyrus buzz."

CHAPTER SIX: THE MAN

"You know," mused Cindy, "the fashion industry is built on women's attempt to be attractive to a partner."

"Don't forget the cosmetic surgery industry," added Clarisse. "And the cosmetic industry."

"Even shoes, fragrances, and jewelry are aimed at attraction and seduction."

"And it's not just women," agreed Clarisse. "Check out men's and little kids' fashions."

"What women think men want from them causes them to go to all sorts of lengths to attract those men—piercings, tattoos, uncomfortable clothing…all in the name of looking hot!"

"It's little wonder women then feel resentful and angry toward men when all this preening doesn't get them the attention they are hoping for," observed Clarisse. "Do you remember your first crush?" she asked Cindy.

"Like it was yesterday!" said Cindy. "His name was Marco and he had that Fonzie black leather jacket look. I thought he was so cool. All the girls in sixth grade had a crush on him."

"You'd vie for being noticed?" Clarisse asked.

"Like a bunch of fighting hell cats," recalled Cindy. "Lisa won his attention. We were too stupid or too naïve to realize it had nothing to do with Lisa. Her dad had season's tickets and Marco had a chance to go to ball games with him."

"We often guess wrong about what men really want, don't we?" Clarisse sighed.

"That sound like the beginning of a sad story," Cindy prodded. "Care to share?"

"I thought my first husband wanted a perfect home, perfect meals, and a wife who greeted him at the door in a fancy dress and high heels. I guess I was affected by episodes of 'Leave it to Beaver' and 'The Ozzie and Harriet Show'. What he really wanted I found out years after our marriage ended was someone to share a drink and ask about his day. But I was too busy lighting the candles and making sure the chateaubriand wasn't overcooked. If I'd just let the meal dry up in the oven or served a casserole that could have waited until he was ready, we'd probably have celebrated our fiftieth anniversary," Clarisse said. "I was too worried about things and not enough concerned about his wants and feelings. I lived up to my image of the perfect wife."

"I'm sure men feel the same way," observed Cindy. "They are so busy working to get us things when what we want most is a warm, romantic partnership. What men think women want from them causes them much the same feelings and frustrations."

"Why don't we ever just level with each other?" Clarisse mused.

"Are you kidding?" exclaimed Cindy. "If we ever did that the fashion industry, the cosmetics industry, the cosmetic surgery industry, the movie industry and even the advertising industry would collapse. Look at how much around us

CHAPTER SIX: THE MAN

is based on the mating ritual! Even the automotive industry would feel the pinch."

"You're right," agreed Clarisse. "The sad part is: It does not have to be this way. If only we'd realize that men and women are human beings first."

"You're right, Clarisse," replied Cindy. "Despite what we think the other person is looking for, we pretty much want the same thing. And we usually don't discover this until it is too late to save that relationship. Then even knowing what we know, we pitch right into the next relationship and make all the same mistakes. Why don't we learn?"

"Are you kidding?" laughed Clarisse. "Divorce lawyers would be bankrupt. Romance writers and the porn industry would be done. The counselling profession would disappear!"

"I never thought about that," Cindy said.

"When I was completing my degree in psychology, I talked to men of various ages and careers about what they wanted in a mate. An overwhelming majority—regardless of age—commented that they were seeking someone who'd communicate with them honestly and openly."

"Wow!" said Cindy. "Think how the way we relate to men would change if we actually heeded this!

"Men want a woman who answers questions honestly. Rather than having women say and do what they think men want, they'd like a woman who even volunteers honest opinions and information. They want a woman who confidently asks for her wants and needs to be met. They want a woman who can see the truth and tell it like it is while still communicating with kindness. Men want a woman who can communicate without being too critical. They want a woman who has dignity and cares about preserving both her dignity and her partner's dignity."

"This sounds a lot like Lady Jane's definition of a lady, doesn't it?" asked Cindy.

"Women think men want them to be superficial, to keep quiet about their needs or wants, and never to ask for anything. Women think men will see them as too needy and too sensitive if they speak up for themselves," Clarisse continued. "Unfortunately women believe they don't have the right to tell the truth. They are afraid they'll be rejected for speaking up."

"Is it because of the way we are raised?" asked Cindy.

"That's part of it," agreed Clarisse. "Whether we like it or not, our mother is our female role model. And our mothers did not often speak up for themselves. They were embarrassed that they had needs and convinced no one wanted to hear about those needs."

"I'm not even sure my mother even acknowledged to herself she had needs," said Cindy. "That generation always put children and spouse first."

"Media has a lot to do with women's self-image too," added Clarisse. "We're shown as part seductress and part servant in advertising."

CHAPTER SIX: THE MAN

"My first real date was my senior prom," Cindy recalled. "I was packaged up like a wedding cake; all ruffles and pink chiffon and curls and carefully minimalist makeup. I was so nervous I was afraid I'd throw up on my date's shoes. Now that I look back on it, he was as scared of making a mistake as I was. We danced like little marionettes and talked about nothing. We never dated again and I am not surprised. Each of us was the other half of the wedding cake topper. It was such a phony situation. After that I decided this boy-girl thing was just too stressful and I went out with a group of friends—none of them date relationships…just a group of friends going to a movie or a concert."

"One of the greatest surprises for me," Clarisse said, "was discovering that men don't find that helpless damsel in distress appealing. Men don't want to be chosen as someone's big brawny hero. That image is far too hard to live up to and downright phony too."

"I watched those little blonds who fluttered their eyelashes and pretended they couldn't open their lockers or carry their own books," agreed Cindy. "Even as boys, the attraction of that type of girl wore off fast. Boys just felt used."

"You're right," said Clarisse. "Those girls might be a big boost to the ego but they weren't lifetime partner material. Men want self-sufficient, secure, confident women as partners. They want a woman who has chosen from desire not desperation. They do not want someone who is financially or emotionally needy. Oh, don't get me wrong," Clarisse added. "Men need to be wanted and needed by their partners. But they want their partners to have their own identity. Men want women who are active and independent. They want their own friends and time to be with those friends. They want women who have their own friends and interests. It's a careful balancing act. They want time to be with their friends but they want time with a loving partner too."

"I remember my first long relationship," Cindy recalled. "Jeff wanted us to spend all our spare time together. I was a cheerleader and on the yearbook club. Jeff would show up for every practice and wait to walk me home. At first all the attention was flattering. But, after a while, it got suffocating. I couldn't go anywhere or do anything without his tagging along."

"How did it end?" asked Clarisse. "Those kinds of relationships seldom end by mutual agreement."

"I got lucky. It was my final year before graduating. I went off to college in another city and Jeff stayed here. We just kind of drifted apart. Jeff has six adorable kids and a wife who hangs on his every word."

"Men want what women want," Clarisse said. "They want an equal partner. I've often told women who are desperately seeking a man to get a life. That may seem harsh but if you build a full, rewarding life of your own, it is surprising how many interesting men you will meet along the way."

"That's how I met Derek," observed Cindy. "I was volunteering at Sunday school when Derek brought his girls to church. I was so impressed at how he handled them. He said he was attracted to me because I was genuinely interested in his girls as people—not a way to gain his notice. After his wife died, there was a whole line of eligible women beating a path to his doorway with casseroles. He felt as if he was being manipulated and—worse—that these women were using his kids as pawns."

"Men don't want to be manipulated. They don't want to have to read a woman's mind or try to interpret signals. Men suck at that and they find it exhausting."

"You're right," Cindy said. "One of the things Derek liked was that I wasn't hunting. Men don't want to be forced to leap into a relationship."

"Right," agreed Clarisse. "They also feel resentful when they are forced to take the blame if a relationship flounders. They don't like end runs played on them."

"Another thing women fail to understand about men is that they don't just want a girl toy or a trophy wife. They actually want us to communicate. Women think men don't want or value praise and acknowledgment. Unfortunately they end up verbalizing criticism. Then we get a reputation for nagging and whining."

"If women would learn that it's not just okay but appreciated that they learn to ask without hesitation for what you want and need, they'd avoid sounding like nags and whiners. We also need to learn how to acknowledge and give praise and a thank you. We're not good at doing either of those things," Clarisse observed.

"Again, doesn't this sound like Lady Jane's lessons about how to act like a lady?" Cindy mused.

"I feel as if the mistakes I made trying to be June Cleaver in my first marriage prepared me for my second marriage," Clarisse admitted. "By then I had figured out that men aren't looking for June Cleaver or Donna Reed. They are looking for Lucille Ball or Clair Huxtable. They want someone honest and forthright. They want a partner who can laugh at herself and have fun. They want someone emotionally stable like Carol Brady, who will share and grow and—yes—even risk making mistakes."

"Wow, Clarisse. That's quite an analogy," said Cindy. "Women think men are in a relationship for the good times. They think men have no interest in a developing and growing a relationship or developing and growing themselves. They think men want women who are super models, Barbie dolls without a response. Actually, they want partners who are emotionally mature, kind, supportive, and loving. In short, men want in women what their fathers have."

"In my third relationship, I learned a valuable lesson," recalled Clarisse. "I realized that maturity doesn't mean not having feelings or not showing your emotions. My third husband was an alcoholic. By bottling up my feelings, I enabled his drinking. I made it easy for him not to get emotionally involved. Emotional maturity means having the ability to handle emotions responsibly. And handling your emotions responsibly doesn't mean hiding them or avoiding expressing them."

"Men don't always give what they want in return," Cindy noted. "Terry demanded fidelity and commitment. However, this didn't stop him from seeking other partners where he also demanded fidelity and commitment. Ironic, isn't it?

CHAPTER SIX: THE MAN

He used to accuse me of having a 'roaming eye' while he virtually undressed every waitress. In the end, he lacked the willingness to work on the relationship. It was as if he always expected the one he was in to fail and he'd have one on the side to fall back on. Our relationship was doomed from the start."

"Your relationship was built on his insecurities just as mine was built on my husband's drinking."

"I feel as if every relationship I've had up to this point has been a dress rehearsal for my marriage to Derek," said Cindy. "Is that horrible?" she asked.

"Not horrible," said Clarisse. "You didn't enter any of those relationships for practice. You entered each hopeful that things were going to work out."

"What if I'm wrong this time?" worried Cindy. "It's not just Derek and me. There are two little girls who have already experienced a loss."

"Think about what Jodi Picoult said in *My Sister's Keeper*," Clarisse reminded Cindy, "'The human capacity for burden is like bamboo- far more flexible than you'd ever believe at first glance.'"

"That's reassuring—but fiction," responded Cindy.

"Kids are a lot more resilient than we give them credit for being," Clarisse pointed out. "Let me just ask you this: However this relationship turns out, would those little girls have been better off not knowing you?"

"You're right. Like their father, those girls need to know I think they are great and I love and appreciate all three of them."

"You bring a unique experience to those little girls and to their father, Cindy," Clarisse pointed out. "I know you don't think you're exceptional. But you are."

When Cindy opened her mouth to protest, Clarisse held up her hand and continued. "You are an original being— hand-crafted by God. He made you with a purpose. You are not an accident of fate or chance. We don't know what His plan is for you and Derek but we do know He has one. You need to trust in His wisdom and be the best mother and partner you can be. God will provide."

"As always, Clarisse," Cindy said, hugging Clarisse, "you know just what to say. How did I ever get so lucky to grow up next to you?"

"God provides what we need when we need it." Clarisse said softly, her eyes glistening with unshed tears.

TAKE A SIP

Love is patient, love is kind. It does not envy, it does not boast, it is not proud. It is not rude, it is not self-seeking, it is not easily angered, it keeps no record of wrongs. Love does not delight in evil, but rejoices with the truth. It always protects, always trusts, always hopes, always perseveres. Love never fails.

Corinthians 13:4-8

SWEET LEMONADE

NOTES:

Chapter Seven:
Managing Finances

There are plenty of ways to get ahead. The first is so basic I'm almost embarrassed to say it: Spend less than you earn.
~Paul Clitheroe

"What's the problem, Cindy?" asked Clarisse. "You look like you've lost your best friend."

Cindy stared glumly at her checkbook ledger. "Try as I might to save money, Clarisse, I always seem to end up broke at the end of the month. Before Derek and I get married I really, really wanted to have my student loans paid off. But every month I end up with nothing extra to put toward them. How do people save money?"

"Well," said Clarisse, "ironically, the people who save money most often are those that already have lots of it. Many people have had lots to say about money and the trouble of having—and not having—it can get us into," remarked Clarisse. "For example, Will Rogers said, 'Too many people spend money they earned…to buy things they don't want… to impress people that they don't like.'"

"And Ralph Waldo Emerson said, 'Money often costs too much.'" Cindy added.

"Dave Ramsey probably gave us the best advice about managing our finances," observed Clarisse.

"What did he say?" asked Cindy.

"'Financial peace isn't the acquisition of stuff. It's learning to live on less than you make, so you can give money back and have money to invest. You can't win until you do this.'"

"That's pretty profound all right," agreed Cindy. "But how do I make this work in real life?" she wailed.

"I have an idea!" exclaimed Clarisse.

"Why am I not surprised?" said Cindy.

Ignoring her sarcasm, Clarisse went on. "A friend runs a series of workshops for people who have money issues. I know I have the information here somewhere," she mumbled rummaging through her huge hand bag. "Aha! Here it is!"

With a flourish, she handed Cindy a flyer. "This looks really helpful but the course starts tomorrow night and it's probably full."

CHAPTER SEVEN: MANAGING FINANCES

"Worth a try," said Clarisse, already dialing. "Mark? It's Clarisse. Yes it has been quite a while…Fine, and you? Mark I have a dear friend who is struggling to pay off her student loans before she gets married. I remembered your financial planning series and wondered if there was room for one more. I'd consider it a personal favor. You do? That's great. Thanks Mark. Her name is Cindy. She'll be there!"

"How do you do that?" asked Cindy.

"Do what?" asked Clarisse.

"Make doors open wherever you go?"

"Oh, Mark's parents are good friends. I helped this with a little problem when Mark was a teenager. Anyhow he has an opening because someone cancelled yesterday. You're in. St. Matthew's church basement. Seven tomorrow night. This is so exciting," enthused Clarisse.

⁓

At exactly 6:55 Cindy pushed open the door of the church basement.

"You must be Cindy," a tall man with a dazzling smile said, shaking Cindy's hand. "Welcome. We're just about to get started."

Cindy looked around. Six others were seated at tables, watching her.

"Rather than starting with those tiresome and embarrassing introductions, we're going to dive right in," announced

Mark. "As the session continues, you'll be doing some activities together and we'll get acquainted that way. You all know I am Mark and if you've read the brochure or visited my website then you know enough about me to know that financial planning is my passion and helping others become better able to manage their finances is a bit of a calling for me. This is not intended to be an economics course. It's just some common sense financial strategies I've helped others learn. Whether you have a little money set aside or you're struggling to get to the end of the month with food still in the fridge, this course is for you. Any questions?" he asked looking at the eight people seated in front of him.

No one said anything.

"Okay then. Let's get started. You should know I am not much of a techno-geek but my son made me this PowerPoint production and you've got to swear you saw it!"

There were smiles and laughs all round.

"Schools do a great job of teaching reading, research and obviously PowerPoint, but personal financial management is not a subject that gets much notice in most schools. It's ironic that a system that teaches advanced mathematical skills most of us will never use unless we're engineers doesn't spend much time on something we all have to deal with in our everyday life. Here goes everybody!"

With a flourish Mark flipped on the projector connected to his laptop. A slide projected on the brick wall. One of the students, a tall bookish looking man with wire rim glasses got up and quietly pulled down the screen so they could see the slide.

"Thanks Paul," said Mark. "You have just become my audiovisual technician. And no one is to tell my son I forgot about the screen."

There were claps for Paul and murmurs of agreement not to tell Mark's son about his faux pas. Paul blushed in embarrassment and smiled shyly at his fellow classmates.

"Here are some statistics," Mark continued as the group looked at the slide.

58% of Americans do not have a retirement plan. They have little or no idea how they'll manage their finances when they get old.

Mark flipped to the next slide and everyone clapped. "Thank you," said Mark, bowing.

People generally believe they'll need about $300,000 to support themselves in retirement. But, the average American has only about $25,000 saved when it's time to retire.

Mark flipped to the next slide:

The average household credit card debt in America is now $15,000.

Mark turned off the machine and said, "If you believe these figures, then you can see why we need to come up with better financial planning. You're all here so I know you're not happy with your financial planning. In a perfect world, what do you hope to get from these sessions?"

Silence greeted his question. Finally a thirty-something blonde spoke up.

"I don't know about the rest of the group but I've got three bright kids and I want to save enough money so they can graduate from college without debts. That's what my parents did for us kids and I figure I owe them that."

Applause greeted her announcement.

"Natalie, that's a great goal. We'll see what we can do to help you save for those kids. How old are they now?" asked Mark.

"Katy is three, Ryan is five and Annalise is seven," responded Natalie.

"That's great. We've got about ten years before Annalise starts college."

"That's why I decided it was time to get started on a college fund," said Natalie. "My parents started a fund for each of them when they were born but I and the kids need to add to that fund."

Cindy responded, "The little girls whose father I am marrying are the same age as your older two, Natalie. I have student loan debts and I want to get those out of the way so I can contribute to the household and the girls' college fund too."

CHAPTER SEVEN: MANAGING FINANCES

"That's a good goal, Cindy," agreed Mark. "It is always better to enter a new relationship debt free. How much do you need to pay off?"

"There's $4,000 left," said Cindy. "I had a good job and managed to pay down a lot of it. But, I've changed jobs. My parents were letting me live with then rent free when I went to school and got started. But, they've retired and moved to Florida. I am buying their old house but it's been a struggle with rent and food and car payments. There's not a lot left at the end of the month."

"Where will you live when you get married?" asked a cute red head.

"I'll be moving in with Derek," Cindy explained. "The girls' school and Derek's work are nearby so it makes sense not to disrupt the girls. They've already had a roller coaster two years with losing their mom. I think my moving in will be the least disturbance to them."

"Well, that's going to eliminate rent, isn't it?" asked Melanie.

"That's a good point," agreed Mark. "But Cindy's immediate financial problem is paying off that $4,000 before the wedding. Am I right, Cindy?"

"Yes," agreed Cindy, "but I'd also like to learn to be better with money so I can help with household money management. My parents have been generous. I pay the utility bills and the taxes on the house. When I move, they will sell it. I want to be in a position like they are when I retire. No debts. Kids through school. Time to travel and enjoy life."

"That's where I want to be," replied a small, slim man with a neatly trimmed beard. "I was a teacher and don't make a lot of money but I do have a good pension. I want to travel and have enough money to enjoy my retirement in five years. And by the way," he added somewhat shyly, "if we had taught financial planning when you were in school, it wouldn't have had much meaning to you. Your parents were paying the bills. It means something now when each of us is facing money concerns. We do teach kids how to create a budget."

"Thanks, Bruce," Mark added. "You make a good point about financial planning. If I'd offered this course when you were sixteen, who of you would have attended?"

Paul raised his hand. The others looked at him.

"I'm a single parent and I have the same worries as Natalie," he explained. "We were young when our kids came along and scraping to get by. I'd like to think I'd have taken your course."

A dark-haired woman in her fifties spoke, here blue eyes sparkling with mirth. "Well I wouldn't have taken the course back then because I thought I knew everything about finances," she said. "Ironically I am the accounts manager for my firm. Handling everyone else's finances is my job. I figured with an MBA handling my own affairs would come naturally. However, I get a lump sum not a pension when I retire and I don't want to spend my retirement years worried about whether I will fall into that group that does not have enough to get by and is forced back into the work force."

CHAPTER SEVEN: MANAGING FINANCES

"Good point, Joan," agreed Mark. "More and more not having a work pension is becoming the norm. We need to figure out how to manage the money we've saved so it allows us a stress-free life."

The attractive red head with the green eyes spoke. "My problem is a little different," she said. "I am a nurse with a good salary and a good pension. However, my mom lives with me. She has health issues which will eventually require a nursing home. Dad didn't leave her with much in the way of a retirement plan and she didn't work outside the home. So basically I need a savings fund that will look after her geriatric care."

"Can't your siblings help out?" asked Natalie.

"I have two brothers with kids to get through school, and mortgages, and car payments," responded Melanie. "They do what they can but their lives are complicated."

"I have trouble just making ends meet," said a strawberry blonde in her mid-thirties. "I'm a cook at a local restaurant. My two teenage boys about eat me out of house and home. I don't have daycare costs anymore and their education is being handled by the armed forces where my husband was a combat pilot. But my day-to-day expenses are mounting and the only way I can get ahead is to work extra shifts and give up time with the boys or look for a better paying job. But I love the Bayside Grill and I don't want to move the boys away from their school and friends."

"Okay. Thanks for your input everyone," said Mark. "I see we all have some immediate or long-term need to save money for kids' college, mother's needs, or our own interests," he concluded. Here's what I want you to do for me. How many of you know where your money goes?"

"Watch my boys eat and you'll get your answer," said Judy.

"I'm going to show you how to create a monthly budget. But before I do that, we need to know exactly where your money went. So everyone copy this form and look at a month's spending…more if you're curious to see trends.

He flashed the next slide:

Monthly Expenses

Rent or mortgage payment

Utilities

Taxes (averaged per month)

Home renovations/repair

Car payments

Car repairs

Car fuel

Groceries

Restaurants

Entertainment

Clothes

Gifts

Savings

Miscellaneous

"Any questions?" Mark asked. "I also want you to do the same thing with this month's spending starting today and keeping track this month. This will be a more accurate account as you're not depending on bills or memory. Once we've figured out where you are spending your money, we can assess where we can trim off to increase savings. Feel free to itemize things individually under miscellaneous and entertainment."

"Mark," said Paul, "Could we do this budget on large sheets so we can hang them up while we share?"

"That's a great idea, Paul. And thanks for not suggesting we do them on PowerPoint."

Everyone laughed.

Paul continued seriously, "Normally I'd suggest that but we want to be able to make comparisons. When you come in next week, I'll do a quick calculation for each of you and we can compare percentages instead of dollar figures so leave the spaces on your large sheet blank beside each item rather than filling in the dollar amount on the big page. Is that okay Mark?"

"That is more than okay, Paul!" exclaimed Mark. "That is inspired!"

Paul mumbled, "Thanks."

"For this month's budget assignment," Mark continued, "don't have to limit yourself. The purpose is just to get an accurate idea of what you spend money on during any given month. Save all your receipts. Make note of how much cash you spend on things like lunch or coffee or parking. Don't forget to add how much is still in your account from this month's salary at the end of the month. Good first session, everyone. See you next Tuesday. Please come a little early if you can so Paul can give you your percent figures."

"Can we send our budget page to him by e-mail so he can do it earlier?" asked Judy.

"Great idea, everyone! On your way out, I'll give you each a card with my email address. Send me your budget page and I'll give you each a copy of everyone's email at our next session….if that's okay, Mark," Paul mumbled.

"It's another inspired idea, Paul!" said Mark.

Everyone filed out picking up a card from Paul on the way.

"How did your first night go?" asked Clarisse over the fence the next day.

"It went great," said Cindy. "The other six people in the

group are really interesting. I know I am going to learn a lot. Thanks for suggesting it," said Cindy. "As always, your ideas are great!"

"What do you have to do for next week?" asked Clarisse.

"I have to look at where I spent my money last month and fill out a form. Then one of the guys is going to convert dollars to percentages so we can talk about each other's spending on a level playing field."

"Great plan," said Clarisse. "Need help?"

"Thanks, Clarisse," Cindy responded. "That would be great!"

"What did we learn from this exercise?" asked Mark after all the budgets were displayed on the wall.

"Paul is great with figures," volunteered Melanie.

"Thanks Paul," the group chorused.

"You're welcome," Paul mumbled, blushing.

"Judy is right," observed Bruce. "Those boys are eating up her income."

"Told you!" Judy replied. "But I've got a sort of solution."

"What?" asked Joan, alarmed. "You're not going to starve them!"

"Better," answered Judy. "I got them a non-paying job five nights a week. Our bus boy quit. We need him only during the lunch and dinner rush. The boys come in after school and work until seven. They don't get paid but when they arrive before the rush, they get whatever they want to eat and they can take home what's left after the rush. The boys are thrilled and my boss loves me. The waitresses even offered to share tips with the boys."

Clapping and whistling followed her announcement.

"What I save on food is going directly into a savings fund for emergencies."

"Cindy is a better saver than she gave herself credit for," noted Joan. "Look at the percentage of her salary she saves."

"Thanks, guys, but it isn't enough in dollars and cents to pay off that $4,000—unless I want to wait until I am forty to get married. So I found a solution too. I am now assisting a wedding photographer on week-ends. In return I am getting a flat fee per wedding and—the best part—she is doing my wedding photographs for free. So I can put that money toward paying off that student loan."

"Seems like many of us have found inspired solutions to our problems," noted Mark.

"I kind of did that too," said Bruce. "I am going to conduct educational tours for the local travel agency. It doesn't pay but all my travel expenses are covered so I travel for free and get to use my history and geography teaching skills too. It was never about money. I just wanted enough to travel and meet people."

Everyone cheered.

"I have some good news too," Melanie offered. "When my brothers heard I was taking this course they asked why. It turns out dad had an insurance policy ear marked for mom's senior care. My brother, the accountant, hadn't thought to mention this because mom hasn't needed it yet. The fund has done pretty well. My brother calculates mom could live to be a hundred and not run out of money."

This news met with hoots and whistles.

"I am going to still save but the new savings will go to trips for mom and me as long as she is able to enjoy them."

"Great news, everyone," said Mark. Here's what I want you to do for next week. Look at the percentages on the budget sheet you've done for tonight. Categorize your purchases budgeting how much of your income you WANT to allocate to each of those items. Make two columns: *projected* budget and *actual* budget. Your projected budget is how much you intend to spend on a category. This is the first step in setting up a monthly budget. Your actual budget is how much you end up spending. It will change from month to month depending on unusual expenses or big ticket items like taxes or insurance. But we're going to spread those expected big ticket items over the year. Don't worry about a column for savings. We're going to keep at least 10% to 15% of total earnings for savings. Remember 100% is what you've got to work with. If a percent is high, do what Melanie, Bruce, and Cindy did. Look for creative ways to pair or supplement that expense. Any questions?"

Everyone was quiet. "Okay then. See you next week. Did you have a suggestion, Paul?" asked Mark.

"Well, yes," answered Paul. "You might like to look at mint.com when you're thinking about creating budgets for next week."

"Another inspired suggestion, Paul," said Mark.

༄

"It's your money," noted Mark, as they began their third session. "There's really no reason to lie to yourself about how much you're going to spend when you're creating a budget. The only person you hurt when you do that is yourself. If you have no idea how you spend your money, your budget may take a few months to gel. Give yourself time to get realistic with yourself."

"I think I have an example," said Joan. "I've budgeted $500 dollars for savings each month. This will consistently stretch my income so, don't put it down. Use a more realistic amount. Then, go back to my budget looking for ways to tweak it or loosen up cash somewhere else, that I can funnel it into savings. Is that right?"

"Exactly right, Joan," said Mark.

"And I should use the same strategy for the fund to pay off the student loan debt?"

"Right, Cindy," agreed Mark.

"Setting a budget will open your eyes to how much money you spend, and where. You may be astonished at the things you discover. Does anyone have an example?" asked Mark.

"Starbucks is not going to be pleased with my discovery," said Joan, "Two hundred dollars a month? Ridiculous!"

"The same goes for me and shoes," added Cindy.

"My vice is movies," said Bruce. "I am renting videos more often from now on."

"My stupid expenditure is gas and parking," commented Natalie. "With public transit too convenient to where I live and work, there is no excuse not to use it. I'm putting that money into a trip for the kids and me."

"By having you look at where your money is going, I didn't mean you needed to give up things you enjoy."

"We know, Mark," commented Paul. "But my $500 for lunches can make a great start on my kids' college fund. I'll pack lunches and go for a walk instead of wasting that time in a noisy, busy restaurant eating food that isn't good for me anyhow. No offense, Judy," Paul said.

"None taken, Paul," answered Judy. "Hey! There are lunch hours I'd rather be brown bagging it in the park, too!"

Everyone laughed. Paul blushed.

"Knowledge is what a budget is about," continued Mark. "It allows you to adjust your spending habits and put the money towards things that are important to you."

"This has been a good activity," said Judy. "I can't wait to discover what new information comes from an accurate accounting this month. Can we compare what we've just done to this month's accounting? Paul, will you do the percentages again?" asked Judy.

"Next week we'll talk about how to plan for the unexpected," said Mark. "Everybody bring in examples of unexpected expenses. And don't forget to keep track of this month's spending every day. Have a good week everyone."

"Anybody wants to come to my house for coffee?" asked Judy. "It's not Starbucks but it's free."

There was a mumble of agreement and most of the group followed Judy to her house.

※

The following week Mark asked how the month's assignment was going.

"I've discovered I should be paying for everything with a credit card. I way undervalued the items I paid for in cash last month," announced Natalie.

There were murmurs of agreement all round.

"That's an important discovery, Natalie," said Mark.

"Why the money I shell out for Pizza Day at school, field trips, and the ice-cream truck, swimming lessons and the like for my kids would feed a third world family!" Natalie said. "Because this is in cash and a few bucks at a time it gets overlooked in budgets unless you are keeping track."

"That was my big discovery this week too, Natalie," said Paul.

"So the kids and I decided to set aside a certain amount per child for those kinds of expenses. If one of them needs extra cash for an unusual expense he can borrow from his brother or get a loan from next month's cash. The kids were as shocked as I was about how much cash gets handed out each month."

"That's a great idea, Natalie," said Paul.

"This week I asked you to think about emergency situations that require quick cash. Let's make a list," said Mark.

"Car breaks down," volunteered Bruce.

Everyone groaned.

"Laid off at work," Joan added.

"Sickness," added Cindy.

"Babysitter quits and there's no one to look after the kids so I miss a day of work," said Melanie.

"Roof springs a leak," added Paul. "House has to have a new roof."

"Those are all good ones," said Mark. "Now the trick to weathering sudden, costly expenses is to plan for the unexpected. Setting a budget will also teach you that you never know when you'll have to pay for something unexpected. That way the unexpected will become expected. You obviously don't plan on your car breaking down, or your child needing medical attention. What you do know is that things like the fridge stopping or the washing machine seizing up are real possibilities. It pays to expect these crises, and to be prepared for them financially."

"So is this like a special savings account for catastrophes, Mark?" asked Cindy.

"That's exactly what it us, Cindy," said Mark.

"I've got one of those," said Bruce. "When I quit smoking everything I saved went there. It's a cushion that has saved me many sleepless nights."

"Next week we are going to talk about when it is better to rent than buy," said Mark. "This week think of some examples."

"Who's for coffee?" called out Judy.

"I brought the coffee this week," said Joan. "It's not Starbucks," she added, "but.."

"It's FREE!" the group shouted.

"Often we buy something that gets used once—or not even that—and it would have been smarter to rent. I asked you for some examples."

CHAPTER SEVEN: MANAGING FINANCES

"DVDs," said Cindy.

"Hockey equipment," added Bruce.

"A place to live," said Melanie.

"My kids' piano," said Natalie.

"Books and magazines," observed Judy, "I should have gotten a library card ages ago."

"A car," added Natalie, "Most times mine sits racking up parking fees. It is easier to walk, bike or take the bus to work and rent a car or hire a cab when I need it."

"Tools," added Paul. "Mine sit and others borrow them."

"Party supplies," added Cindy. "It's far cheaper to rent equipment you're going to use at most once a year."

"Or rent the party package at Chuck E Cheese or McDonalds or the bowling alley," added Judy.

"Everyone says rent is lost equity," observed Paul. "But home ownership is expensive."

"I rent all my sporting equipment," added Joan. "Skis, golf clubs, tennis racquet, bowling ball…I don't use any of them enough to make owning worth the cost, the upkeep and the storage."

"Joan has made a good point. If you're going to use an item enough that it is worth the investment, the upkeep, and the storage then it's worth owning."

"Sometimes, like my kids' piano, it would have been so much cheaper and easier to rent," noted Natalie.

"I'm renting my wedding dress," said Cindy. "This course has taught me it is the way to go."

"Next week is our last session," Mark concluded at the end of the discussion. We'll take a look at our final budget assignment and talk about what we learned. Any questions?"

"I have one," said Bruce. "Who is coming to Judy's house. Coffee is on me. It's…"

"NOT STARBUCK'S BUT IT'S FREE!" the group shouted in unison.

"I baked a coffee cake," announced Paul.

"Why Paul," said Judy, "You have another hidden talent! Why hasn't some woman scooped you up ages ago?"

"Maybe they've met my kids," Paul mumbled, blushing.

It was the group's last night. Everything had taken on a festive air. The group had decided to meet at six for a potluck before the class. A large coffee urn stood in the middle of the buffet table. On it was a sign:

CHAPTER SEVEN: MANAGING FINANCES

It's not Starbucks, but it's FREE! Everyone enjoy!

There was a warm camaraderie as the class convened. Everyone had exchanged phone numbers and promised to keep in touch.

"We've talked of many things," Mark began. "You've all created a budget to guide your finances. You've tweaked it based on what you discovered in your second assignment. Let's look at what we've learned."

"Paul's coffee cake rocks," said Melanie.

"Get Paul's recipe," added Cindy.

"Get Paul!" said Judy. Paul blushed.

"How about some financial discoveries?" asked Mark. "I'm going to write them down. Just call them out as fast as I can get them jotted down."

"Knowledge is power. Know where your money is going," said Judy.

"Have a special account for unexpected emergencies," said Bruce.

"Before you buy think about whether renting or borrowing is a better way to go," added Natalie. "I have a piano for sale or rent."

Everyone laughed.

"Spend what you have, not what you hope to make. Unless it's an emergency, only spend money that you have, not money that you expect to make. Borrow only in a crisis like emergency repairs or illness or a roof over your head," said Paul.

"When you're strapped for cash look for creative solutions like having your kids work for food, or carpooling, or swapping babysitting," said Bruce.

"Try to save 10 to 20% of what you earn," said Melanie.

"Before you buy something—like those red shoes—ask yourself if this is a wise purchase," added Cindy.

"Thanks guys," said Mark. "Your participation has made this a valuable learning experience. My next course is on how to make your savings work for you. I have brochures at the door if you or anyone you know might be interested. The course will look at stock market and real estate as well as such things as life insurance, health insurance, homeowner's insurance, disaster insurance, and saving for retirement."

"How much do we need to take the next course, Mark?" asked Joan.

"Nothing, Joan," said Mark. "This is an information course. I'm not here to sell you real estate."

"Count me in," said Judy. "That is if Paul is baking!"

"You're on!" said Paul.

Many of the group murmured in agreement.

CHAPTER SEVEN: MANAGING FINANCES

"Last but not least," said Mark, "I bring you this announcement from my son."

He flipped on the slide projector. On the screen appeared a younger version of Mark.

"Hey guys," said the younger version of Mark. "My name is Michael. Sorry I didn't get a chance to meet each of you. My dad has talked nonstop about you these past few weeks. Perhaps I'll get a chance to meet you at the next course. You're coming aren't you? I prepared a finale slide presentation on money management and I've sent it to each of your email addresses. Thanks for helping my dad get over his technophobia. A special thanks to you, Paul for the email addresses and for being my dad's technical advisor."

Paul blushed.

A final screen came up. It read:

A good financial plan is a road map that shows us exactly how the choices we make today affect our future.
~Alexa Van Tobel

SWEET LEMONADE

TAKE A SIP

It's your turn. Take charge of your finances!

BUDGET WORKSHEET

Category	How Often	Monthly Budget Amount	Monthly Actual Amount	Difference
INCOME				
INCOME SUBTOTAL				
EXPENSES				

CHAPTER SEVEN: MANAGING FINANCES

EXPENSES SUBTOTAL					
NET INCOME (Income − Expenses)					

NOTES:

Chapter Eight:
Build Your House

Therefore everyone who hears these words of mine and puts them into practice is like a wise man who built his house on the rock. The rain came down, the streams rose, and the winds blew and beat against that house; yet it did not fall, because it had its foundation on the rock. But everyone who hears these words of mine and does not put them into practice is like a foolish man who built his house on sand. The rain came down, the streams rose, and the winds blew and beat against that house, and it fell with a great crash.
~Matthew 7:24-27

"You look worried, Cindy," observed Clarisse. "Surely it's not wedding plans that are concerning you. You've got everything planned down to minute details."

"No Clarisse. It's not that. I'm worried about after the wedding."

"Oh. I see," said Clarisse thoughtfully. "The honeymoon has you feeling nervous?"

"No it's not that either," said Cindy. "It's being part of a family and making sure I am good for Derek's girls. Their mother did so much to make their home warm, inviting, and safe. I want the girls to have that same sense of safety and protection my parents gave me. I've thought and thought about how they did that and frankly I am stumped. I'm not just imagining that feeling of home being a haven, am I Clarisse?"

"No, dear," said Clarisse. "You're not imagining things. Your parents worked hard to make their children feel cherished, safe, and confident."

"And I didn't always make it an easy task, did I?" asked Cindy, wiping away a tear. "When I think of what I put my parents through, I am sad and embarrassed," she admitted.

"Well Cindy," said Clarisse, "they never tried to give you away. When things were tough I reminded them of what my grandmother used to say: 'If they never make you cry then they'll never make you laugh either.'"

"How will I ever make Derek's girls feel safe, happy, and confident?" asked Cindy.

"It's no easy feat to be a good parent, Cindy. But, you're well on your way."

"How so?" asked Cindy. "You'd hardly call my first attempt at parenting a huge success."

CHAPTER EIGHT: BUILD YOUR HOUSE

"Yes I would call that a success," insisted Clarisse. "You did what was best for that baby given the circumstances and some couple is over the moon to have him in their lives."

"But, that doesn't help me figure out how to make a happy home for Derek and the girls and future children," sighed Cindy.

"I have an idea," said Clarisse, snapping her fingers.

"Really?" said Cindy drily.

"My friend Lilly teaches a course at our church. She calls it "Building your House upon a Rock". It's based on the scripture Matthew 7 verses 24 to 27. She teaches couples how to build a strong family relationship which will withstand the storms of life."

"Do you think she'd let me sit in?" asked Cindy.

"I'm sure she would," said Clarisse. "I'll call her right away."

Cindy looked around her. The church auditorium was full. There must have been a hundred people in attendance. They all looked worried. Cindy knew how they felt. She was lucky. When Clarisse phoned, Lilly assured her there was always "room for one more" and the first session of this course started the following week. So they were all newbies.

A small woman with her gray hair in a bun at the base of her neck rose from the front row. She was wearing a long skirt printed with white and yellow daisies, and Birkenstocks. Her blue sleeveless top matched her sparkling eyes.

She tapped the microphone gently and said, "Good evening everyone. I'm Lilly- of-the-valley and, yes, my parents were hippies."

A chuckle rippled through the crowd. Everyone relaxed just a little.

"When we were kids home was our refuge, our sanctuary. This is no longer the case. Now it is place of noise and bills and constant interruptions from the television, phones, iPods, email, and streamed movies. Think of the last time your house was perfectly quiet. The outside world is constantly infringing on our personal family space."

A hand was raised hesitantly.

"Yes Ralph," said Lilly.

"Um I'm wondering what electronics have to do with building a secure home where our kids feel safe and loved."

"That is an excellent question," commented Lilly.

Cindy was glad Ralph had asked it because she wanted to know too.

"In order to feel secure," Lilly continued, "we all need a safe place to come home to. We need a place that makes us feel physically and emotionally secure."

CHAPTER EIGHT: BUILD YOUR HOUSE

A pretty red head raised her hand. "Hi, everyone, I'm Melanie. I'm not sure if you want us to talk but I have something to add that might help."

"Welcome, Melanie," said Lilly. "Please share!"

"When I was growing up there were seven of us. The house was always full of us and our friends. There was never a moment of quiet. I used to do my homework under the basement steps because it was the only place that was close to quiet. I never felt secure. I used to long to be an only child where you could hear the clock ticking and the sound of the crickets outside the window."

"You're right, Melanie," responded Lilly. "I too had one of those constantly in a turmoil homes. My parents were always letting some friend or another crash at their place. It was my birthday and I'd baked cupcakes for the kids in my class. Their friends had a party and ate my cupcakes. My parents didn't even remember it was my birthday. Kids have enough demands just growing up. They need a secure, solid home where they feel sheltered from all that confusion in the outside world and protected. They need to feel that their parents can keep them safe: from the neighborhood bully, from kidnappers, from terrorists, from their friends trashing their house and eating their cupcakes. Modern technology has made kids all too aware of the dangerous situations out there in the world. To quote my daughter, kids need a 'hidey hole'."

"Can I add something?" asked a tall man in a nicely tailored suit.

"Please do, Andrew," invited Lilly.

"No matter how independent we seem to be at work or school, we all need to know that we can count on someone—whether it is our parents, a spouse, our kids or a friend or relative—when we get home. That is what makes home a haven. There is someone waiting for you there. My parents both worked long hours but my grandma was always right across the street with ice cold milk and chocolate chip cookies. Today I still associate chocolate chip cookies with a sense of security."

"In spite of their efforts to appear cool in front of their friends, your children would rather be with you than anywhere else in the world for a very long time. Even after they start going to sleepovers and birthday parties, when they come home, they want two things: a safe place to be themselves without worrying about what others think, and to connect with the rest of the family—even though they claim to hate their siblings," said Lilly. "If kids seem glued to the TV screen time, their phone or the computer, you need to reach out to them."

Cindy raised her hand. "I agree with Lilly. I was one of these teenagers who professed to hate my family and live for my friends. I was grateful my parents took the phone and the computer away and spent time with me. It made me feel I was worth the bother. Giving your children a sanctuary is a huge gift. It gives kids a place to let down their public persona, relax, and recharge. Now I appreciate the effort my parents made. I want to create that same sense of family culture. I want to make home a cozy nest where my new daughters can thrive. That's why I'm here. To figure out how my parents did that."

CHAPTER EIGHT: BUILD YOUR HOUSE

"Thanks Cindy," said Lilly. "Research shows that adults who purposely set out to create homes that are nurturing and beautiful report better moods and less stressful lives."

"So what can we do to create a sanctuary for our family?" asked a man with a black beard.

"Good question, Brian," said Lilly. "Let's brainstorm. Think of what your home offered if it was nurturing and what you wish it had been like if it lacked that comfortable, secure feeling."

"Slow things down," called out one voice.

"Please explain, Mark," said Lilly writing: Slow down on the white board.

"Just like someone said things were never quiet, we're involved in too many things. We're never home as a family. Someone has a lesson, or a game, or a school activity every night. I want off the merry-go-round. We need to take a breath!"

Mark's speech met with thunderous applause.

"We all love excitement," agreed Lilly. "But stress kills… literally. Stress wears on our patience, our health, and our good humor. Stress makes us irritable and more likely to become angry over stupid little things. We make our lives more stressful than they need to be, simply by not slowing down. We've got ourselves into too many things because we can't say no and we don't want to miss out on anything!"

"Treat each other with respect," added another voice.

"How can we do that, Mary?" Lilly asked writing down: Treat each other with respect.

"No violence, physical or verbal, no fighting or bickering or hitting. My parents were verbally and physically abusive to one another and later to us. I vowed I'd never make my kids feel the way I felt at home."

"Try not to make everything so structured no one can relax," volunteered a man.

"Can you elaborate, Fred?" asked Lilly writing down: *Avoid too much structure.*

"I know what you said about kids needing structure to feel secure but they also need their home to be low-pressure, not a performance. My parents were both physicists. Everything was a test or a report or an assignment. Kids need to be contributing members of the household. But they don't need to feel as if everything they do is being evaluated. Kids also need plenty of time to chill out. We were buried in too many obligations on top of homework, basic chores, and music practice. We were under tremendous stress."

"Let your kids show their bad side," said a woman. "All day long they show their public face—the one you want the crowd to see. Cut them some slack to be whiny, or petulant, a bit childish no matter how old they are. They need a safe place to let their hair down…just as Fred was pointing out. All kids need a chance to be their baby self. If they get this chance they're less likely to disintegrate into a crying

CHAPTER EIGHT: BUILD YOUR HOUSE

puddle or throw a temper tantrum in line at the supermarket or at Grandma's house for dinner."

"Been there!" piped up a voice.

The crowd laughed.

"Sadly those Baby Selves will disappear sooner than you can imagine—along with your car keys!" said a middle-aged man.

"I understand kids needing space and security to show their true selves," said Lilly. "And I get where Fred and Rhonda are coming from about too much structure in the house. However, I stand by what I said about kids needing routines and predictability too. Kids need to know what is expected of them and what to expect from those around them. Imagine yourself sitting working on a landscaping project. Your spouse announces that her parents will be coming for a visit the next day. They're staying two weeks and no one has thought it important to tell you this. Would you feel as if you had no control over the next fourteen days? This is the way kids often feel. They have little control over their lives. Springing unscheduled changes on them makes them feel they have no control and they often push back. This resistance is their way to try to get some control over a life they feel is rolling around like tumbleweed. Structure keeps things more organized. Predictable routines eliminate the stress of constant last-minute changes and searches for things."

"Turn off the technology," called out a voice.

This met with loud applause.

"Yeah? You clap, but how many of you enforce the no technology at the table rule?" she asked. "I feel like the meanest mom in the world because I won't let my kids text, email, send or receive phone calls during dinner. They've told their friends that they are a blacked out zone during dinner and homework."

"We need to set a good example for our kids by turning off the tablet, the laptop, the computer and the cell phone to spend time with the family. I'm a mean parent too. Not only is our house a blacked out zone over dinner, it's a family rule that Saturdays are technology-free."

Huge applause met this announcement. "Yeah? Well now go home and do it," challenged a sandy-hair man in his forties. "If YOU are worried about how you'll cope, it's a sure sign that your house needs a scheduled weekly tech-free day. Try it. Honestly? You'll live through it and get to know your family into the bargain!"

A small dark-haired woman put up her hand.

"Yes Larissa," said Lilly.

"I'm an oncologist. I'd just like to point out what a powerful tool silence or soft relaxing natural sounds like waves or birdsongs are. I've done some research on white noise. We have it in every room of our house as well as my office. I've done extensive research on the power of peaceful sounds for relieving stress and nourishing your immune system—and your soul. The other side of this coin is that our society is too loud: blaring TV, upsetting news, and honking squealing traffic. My friends who come to visit me from the city

CHAPTER EIGHT: BUILD YOUR HOUSE

can't stand the quiet. They need city noises to be able to sleep. All this noise isn't healthy. We need to slow down and quiet down our homes. They did a study of companion dogs. The ones who lived in cities had shorter lives because of the noise stress. Anything we can do to minimize noise in our homes will protect our family both physically and emotionally."

"That's good information, Larissa. Thanks for that," replied Lilly.

"Can I add something," a small East Indian man added shyly.

"Of course Vijay," said Lilly.

"Our kids need a supportive family culture," he said. "I'm a child psychologist and I see the effects of a lack of family culture."

"Can you explain how we can develop a family culture?" asked Lilly.

"It's a way to hold your family together and make them a unique unit. It has little to do with your ethnic origins and more to do with an identifier like the Smith family that step dances together or the Avrils family who bike on week-ends or the Williams who regularly take cruises or the Watsons who do tai chi together or the camping Andersons. Do you get my point?" asked Vijay looking around at the crowd. Several nodded their understanding.

"Yours might be an athletic family or history buffs or a family that cooks together. Maybe you're a family of readers or ventriloquists."

"Our family hosts kid's backyard camp overs," said Larissa. "Is this part of a family culture?"

"I've always thought eating dinner together was an important part of being a family," added petite, blond Emily.

"You're right!" agreed Vijay. "With everything families have going on it's hard to do this but well worth the effort."

"My family grazed," said Lilly. "I always envied kids whose mothers cooked a real meal and everyone sat around the table talking about their day. I used to love to go to my friend, Jennifer's, house because that's what they did."

"I used to gripe about our parents insisting we be home for dinner," laughed Doris. "Then I did the exact same thing with my kids. By then I realized that over the dinner table is where family members commiserate over skinned knees and snubs on the playground and not making the cut for sports teams. It's also where families mark milestones, share dreams, bury sibling grudges, make compromises, celebrate successes, plan vacations, and tell jokes. It's also where children learn the lessons that families teach: manners, cooperation, communication, self-control, and values. Following directions. Sitting still. Taking turns. It's where kids learn to be part of a family and how to parent their own."

"Dinners together can change a kid's life," Cindy observed. "When I was a rebellious, drug-using teenager, my parents insisted that we have dinner together as a family. That ritual, believe it or not, kept me grounded. It must have been hard for them because making conversation with me was like pulling teeth."

CHAPTER EIGHT: BUILD YOUR HOUSE

"Dinner is the best predictor of how kids will do in adolescence," said Vijay. "Research has shown that the more frequently kids eat dinner with their families, the better they do in school, and the less likely they are to become sexually active, suffer depression, get involved with drugs or alcohol, or consider suicide. It's amazing, isn't it?" he added. "But it's just like Cindy pointed out. That ritual keeps kids grounded in their family culture."

"I think it's also because parents who make it a priority to show up and eat with their kids are more likely to express their love constructively in other ways. Kids are getting attention and supervision," pointed out Doris. "Families who offer kids more structure are more likely to monitor their kids' homework and make sure things are going well at school."

"Wow! That's a lot of mileage for family dinners, isn't it?" exclaimed Cindy.

"Yes," agreed Vijay. "Perhaps it is because dinner takes individual family members out of being single units and into being part of a group. This gives parents more of the same power of the kids' peer group."

"Speaking as one who did not have this family ritual and envied it in other kids," added Lilly, "I think it's so powerful because children, even more than the rest of us, need something to count on every day. They need a tangible security of belonging and being nurtured. Sharing food in a social setting with people we love and whom we know love us is a strong part of the family fabric."

"No offense, Lilly. I know you didn't have this ritual and I'm not finding fault with your parents but I feel strongly that a family who shares dinner time is a pretty easy insurance to build into your home life. If you're too busy to have dinner as a family on a regular basis, then, as a parent you may want to re-examine your priorities," said Doris.

"I couldn't agree more, Doris," responded Lilly. "I always felt I was missing out on something important."

"Obviously, it's ideal if both parents can have dinner with their kids every night. But we don't live in a perfect world. So we do the best we can. Given work schedules, travel and commutes, this may mean one parent is there for many weeknight dinners but it is even more important, then, that the other parent is there for week-end dinners. It's all the more important that the whole family have time together on the weekend. Sharing meals together is an outstanding way to build family identity," Vijay pointed out.

"My kids have sports which often get in the way of dinner together," said Susan. "We were going every which way every night with two or three kids in events that overlapped. I felt like the chauffeur and we certainly weren't eating right. That's when we had a family meeting and decided that some things had to go so good eating habits, sleep times, and homework didn't suffer. Surprisingly, when we pared things down, the kids were relieved! They felt over extended too. There is too much of a good thing," offered Wayne.

Wendy added, "We have another problem. My kids feel resentful and pouty when I don't let them eat in front of the

CHAPTER EIGHT: BUILD YOUR HOUSE

TV. They insist it is still family time if we all eat together in the TV room instead of the kitchen. Does that count?"

"Let me ask you this," posed Lilly. "Does it make you feel more connected to your family?"

"Not as much as a conversation around the kitchen table," admitted Wendy.

"Then I think you have your answer," Lilly responded. "It's challenging to make dinner fun and relaxing when everyone is pressured and tired and the TV is blaring in the background. It's also a lot easier to turn on the TV than to interact with your kids. Eating in front of the TV builds your relationship with the TV, not with each other."

"I'm a horrible mom," wailed Jennifer, "but after work and my long commute,

I'm so wiped out at the end of the day that I don't have the energy to make dinner into anything special."

Lilly nodded. "I know just how you feel, Jennifer. "After work schedules, what to feed your family is the single biggest obstacle to family dinners."

"I've got a solution for that," piped up Tammy. "This isn't a wedding banquet or dinner for the in-laws. My secret is to minimize the cooking. Over complicating things just stresses you and the kids. At our house, we take a few minutes at breakfast to talk about the next six days' dinners. Kids get to suggest what we have. Then we create a list. Kids scamper to the cupboard to see if we need specific ingredients.

When it is your menu it is also your job to set the table and help with preparations. The other kids are responsible for clean-up. That way the whole meal is a shared family thing. We also have Saturday work bees where we get desserts for school lunches made and frozen in individual bags for the following week and things like chili, meat loaf, stews and casseroles are made ahead."

"Those are great suggestions," noted Vijay. "Dinner is so important to me as a foundation for family culture. It is a cherished family tradition. I'd rather skimp somewhere else, if I have to.

"My kids are teenagers," said Valerie. "They want to be out with their friends on week-ends but they're fine with family dinners on week nights. Is it okay to bend on this?" asked Marilyn.

"If you have dinner as a family most other nights, I see nothing wrong with giving them Saturday night. It can be treated as "party night" for everyone," said Lilly .This gives you and your mate a dated night or a movie night or a romantic dinner evening."

"I've made a twist to that date night," said a vivacious woman. "On Saturday nights, I open my house to my kids' friends for dinner. It's nothing fancy or complicated: homemade stew, lasagna and a salad, chili and chips, burgers and salads…Many of the kids are now bringing a loaf of homemade bread or a dessert from their grateful parents. We sit around and discuss the week or upcoming events before the kids head out to a movie or a party. The kids all think we are cool. Our kids have even begun to think so!"

CHAPTER EIGHT: BUILD YOUR HOUSE

"Wow, Connie," what a great gesture.

Everyone applauded.

"It's selfish on my part," Connie said. "I know where my kids are. I know they are eating right. I know who their friends are and what's going on in their world."

"I've found a solution for that walk in the door and everyone is expecting dinner thing," volunteered Suzanne. "Like the Italians, our house has an antipasto course. While we're getting dinner, setting the table, one of the kids puts out healthy snacks: carrots and hummus, Pita chips, fruit, cheese and crackers. We all nibble and have a beverage and take ten before getting dinner on the table and sitting down. We're all in better humor because of it."

"We start our meal with a brief gratitude statement from each of us," commented Beryl. "Then we sing the Johnny Appleseed grace and dig in."

"That's a great family tradition!" exclaimed Connie. "I'm going to start doing that with my Saturday Friends and Family dinner."

"Wonderful idea, Beryl," enthused Lilly. "The attitude of celebration and appreciation is one of the greatest things we can bring to family dinners. As parents we need to set the tone by overlooking trivial things like not-quite-perfect table manners and focus instead on what really matters."

Food is only secondary to family dinners," added Connie. "The point of sitting down to dinner is to connect with each other. I fuss with a roast and all the trimmings for Sunday dinner and often invite the kids' grandparents. But, I rarely knock myself out with anything elaborate when it's just our family eating together during the week. Keep it simple. Save your energy for making the dinner a pleasant time, rather than cooking a meal that leaves you exhausted—and the kids won't like it anyhow."

Larissa laughed and added, "I am the queen of ten meals centered around spaghetti with sauce from a jar and salad from a bag. Well I do add my own cucumbers, peppers, and tomatoes."

"I often throw together an omelet with some creative ingredients like cheeses and vegetables and some leftover chopped meat. We sometimes build our own pizzas from purchased dough and ingredients like ham, pineapple, black olives, diced chicken, grated cheese and ground pre-cooked meat. Kids like that and clean-up is easy," offered Mary. "I used to run a restaurant so I know how to do simple stuff kids love. I am an artist with grilled sandwiches."

"I'm writing this all down," said Cindy.

"Build rituals into your dinner. Like taking turns having a funny story to tell or being in charge of selecting background music or choosing the dessert or asking the blessing or picking a topic of conversation. It makes kids feel a part of the family project and adds predictability to the meal," suggested Vijay.

"By taking turns choosing a topic for discussion, the dinner conversation is not limited *to just* adults talking about their

CHAPTER EIGHT: BUILD YOUR HOUSE

jobs. There's something for kids to learn hearing sometimes about their parents' days as well as their own. At our house, we usually start with a quick check-in round of: How was school/work today?" said Mary.

"We do that too. But, we use what was said. For example: Science Fair Project as a springboard to: What are you considering? And talk about other science fair projects, or steps of the project or materials/help needed. We've never had trouble finding a topic of conversation. It's also important for kids to be a part of family decision and we do that over dinner. Sometimes our discussions turn to current events," offered Cliff.

"We try to have something to celebrate every day," said Suzanne. "Sometimes it's who got the best paper or who cleaned up his room fastest or who was the most help getting dinner or who made up the best verse to a silly song or who put away groceries the fastest. We try to have fun together every day because the family that laughs together builds relationships that sustain them during the hard times."

"I'd love to hear what your family does to have fun," Cindy said. "I'm new to this mother thing and I really want the girls to feel that their family is fun."

"I too inherited a ready-made family. Things were a bit rocky on the start," Suzanne said. "I found that silliness and humor could smooth over the rough spots and keep everyone smiling. Children whose parents use silliness to keep the day flowing smoothly often have less stress.

At first, I found that unless I made instructions into a game, the boys were so wrapped up in TV or their video games that unless I wanted to become a tyrant, they wouldn't even notice me. I did all sorts of strange things like dressing in an ape costume and *announcing "Little Monkeys, it's time for breakfast. Come and eat your bugs and bananas!"* and *"Don't you think your steam shovel wants to get in the car now so he can see the construction site on the way to the store?"* rather than snarling: *"Eat your breakfast now!"* and *"Get in the car!"*

"Wow! You did that?"

"Yes. I was a legend in the neighborhood. I am convinced that creating fun traditions gives your family something to look forward to. Make anything into a game."

"How?" asked Cindy, her pencil poised.

"I use funny voices and masks and funny glasses and wigs. Try trading roles at the dinner table. Everybody acts like someone else. Watching the kids portray adults is hilarious. Have a race to get dressed or into bed for story time. Make a game of doing houschold cleanup together. Create silly song lyrics in the car. Have a tickle contest. End the day with a pillow fight. Play noncompetitive games where anyone can win."

"Like what?" asked Cindy.

"Relay-Race" Jammies is one of our favorites," answered Suanne. "One child takes off one piece of clothing, runs to another room, and touches a certain spot and then runs back, takes off the next item or puts on the next bed-time item, and then repeats until he is dressed—or undressed and into his PJs. This gets rid of the evening energy and takes

CHAPTER EIGHT: BUILD YOUR HOUSE

the focus off the chore of getting ready for bed. We follow this with a quiet activity like a bedtime story."

"That's great!" replies the enthused Cindy. "The girls hate getting ready for bed."

"We have trouble with kids who don't like seatbelts," added Emma. "So we play airplanes. Pretend you are going on an airplane. You be the flight attendant, saying, *"Flight 1234 will begin boarding in five minutes. Please collect your baggage and proceed to the gate."* Then when they're in the car announce, *"All ticketed passengers should now be on board."* Once in the "airplane" the flight attendant asks all passengers to make sure their seatbelts are buckled *"low and tight across their laps"*. You *"prepare for takeoff"* on the driveway and off you fly. This saves my harping at them to get into the car and buckle up."

"We play fireman when we are pressed for time. I ring the alarm and we all scoot to see how fast we can be dressed and ready in the fire engine," said Suzanne.

"Good one!" said Emma. "Can I use that one?"

"I'll never be as creative as you two," moaned Cindy.

"Yes you will," assured Suzanne. "It's called survival. Go with the ideas you've been given and new ones will occur to you!"

"Kids will invent games, too," said Emma. "My son invented this game. The parent tells the child I don't think you can do..........Then the parent acts surprised when it happens. Like you say, "Now how did those clothes get in the hamper?" or "Where's the magic fairy that cleaned this room?" or "How did those dishes get into the dishwasher?"

"Kids love to be timed," said Suzanne. "Use a stopwatch to see how long it takes your children to do a task like cleaning up his toys. Then say, "Wow! 3 minutes and 9 seconds!"

"I play the Jeopardy song while kids pick up toys or put dirty clothes in the hamper or stack the dishwasher. That works well too," said Emma. "The kids even hum it while they are packing their backpacks."

"Pamela and Becky and I have races getting dressed," said Cindy.

"I tell the kids, 'We can do it together, because we're a 'Can-Do Team!'" said Suzanne. "The kids help each other get dressed, brush teeth, get breakfast, pack backpacks, and load the car. I cheer them on. I try to develop this Can-Do Team attitude toward everything. Everything is a team effort. We all share ideas and suggestions about how best to accomplish something. When something breaks down, the whole team stops what they're doing and problem solves."

"Kids love to do other people's chores," observed Emma. "We play a game called Top-to-Bottom Cleanup. We all work together to clean the house. The laundry basket is a dump truck and the vacuum is a bulldozer. When we're done we go through the rooms noting how clean they are and how great it feels to work together."

"It is important to share each other's interests," added Mary. "Believe me this is not always a walk in the park! One of my

CHAPTER EIGHT: BUILD YOUR HOUSE

sons is a snake enthusiast and quite frankly snakes make me want to run screaming from the yard. But he's fascinated by them so I share his passion as he shares mine for books and antique shopping. I've also learned more than I thought possible about Star Wars trivia and Barbie. Taking an interest in your kids' passions lets you find out all sorts of things about their hopes and fears.

"I work at having a comfortable, loving, kid-oriented tone in our house," commented Jill. "My mother was a successful interior decorator. Our house always looked like a page from Better Homes and Gardens or Architectural Digest. Her house was a working set and we were expected to float above the white carpet. There were five bathrooms in our house but the only one we were allowed to use was on the third floor of our house where clients never ventured. We used to call ourselves the attic children. I don't want that kind of tension for our kids. I want them to feel that their home is like a comfortable pair of old slippers."

"Kids need space and security to be themselves," agreed Suzanne. "My father was British and viewed kids as short adults. Our house always felt like an English boarding school when he was home. He didn't understand that kids are more physical than adults. When they get wound up emotionally, their bodies need to discharge all that energy. That's one of the reasons they wear us adults out. My mom understood this. She played physical games with us. We used to giggle and sweat and scream. It was a great way to discharge positively. I am convinced she avoided a lot of the temper tantrums we see kids throwing simply because all that built up energy has to go somewhere."

"Your mother was wise," commented Lilly. "Playing is also how kids learn. As adults when you "teach" an emotional lesson by playing, your child really gets it. Best of all, playing helps you and the kids feel closer."

"At the end of the day, parents are exhausted," commented Connie. "The last thing we feel like doing is playing an active game. The good news is that these games don't last long—maybe ten minutes, or even as little as two minutes. For all the benefits they bring they are time well spent. And, surprisingly you will feel less exhausted after playing with your kids."

"Play with our kids is re-energizing because the tension and irritation we carry around with us all day makes us tired. When we play, we discharge stress hormones just like our kids, giving us more energy," commented Vijay.

"Play is important but don't overlook the importance of snuggling time too," Alice pointed out. "My parents were not touchy feely sorts. I longed for kisses and hugs and even pats on the head. Kids feel protected when they can sink into the comfort of your lap. When kids of any age are hurting they need a hug and someone to rock them in their arms."

"This is all very helpful," said Cindy. "Can I ask a question? My new daughters-to-be have had a very challenging year. They lost their mother and will soon get a new person in their house and they will be starting back to school. That's a lot for two little girls to deal with. How can I help?"

Vijay said, "Role play with stuffed animals is a good way to help your child discuss big issues like starting school or the

CHAPTER EIGHT: BUILD YOUR HOUSE

loss of a pet or the death of someone close to them. To help a child who's coping with a challenging issue, like the start of school, or a bully on the playground or a new person in their household, try having one stuffed animal be the parent, and one be the child, and act out the situation. Using stuffed animals removes the issue or concern one step real life. Most kids find it more comfortable. Some kids like to actually act out the situation themselves. Playing out these situations that cause so much stress for kids helps them to feel more in control of their own emotions, and lets them be the powerful one in a situation where they might have felt powerless in real life."

"Well, it looks as if our time is up for tonight. We've roamed far away from the topic of building a solid home for ourselves and our families. However, everything we've discussed has been aimed at providing a warm, comfortable, confidence-building home for our families. I hope you are all taking away something useful that will help you make your house a haven, a refuge for your family. Cindy, you've been writing like mad all evening. Would you care to share your thoughts?" asked Lilly.

"Actually I'd like that," commented Cindy. "I'd like to get input from others about things I might have missed or misinterpreted. I was writing pretty fast."

"As you read, I'll write the main points on the white board so we can see them," said Lilly.

Cindy began to read and Lilly started writing:

Cindy's Notes: Building a Strong House

Our home was our refuge, our sanctuary. Now it is place of noise and bills and constant interruptions.

We need a place to come home to where we feel physically and emotionally secure.

Houses with lots of noise or constant turmoil do not make us feel secure.

Kids need to feel that their parents can keep them safe: from the neighborhood bully, from kidnappers, and cupcake stealers (-:

Modern technology has made kids all too aware of the dangerous situations. Kids need to feel home is their hidey hole.

No matter how independent we seem we need someone to count on—parents, spouse, kids, friend, relative. Home needs to be a safe haven.

Children would rather be with you than anywhere else—even if it's not cool to admit this.

We are the glue that holds family together.

It's important for parents to take the phone and the computer away and spend time with kids. It makes kids feel they matter.

Research** adults who purposely set out to create homes that are nurturing and beautiful report better moods and less stressful lives.

How to Build a Nurturing Home

1. Slow things down—don't try to be involved in everything.

2. Treat each other with respect—No violence, physical or verbal, no fighting or bickering or hitting.

3. Avoid too much structure. Kids also need time to chill out—relieve stress, and be themselves.

4. Everyone also need routines and predictability. Kids need to know what is expected of them and what to expect from others.

5. No technology at the table rule. Talk to one another!

6. Power of quiet and soothing background music—research* power of peaceful sounds for relieving stress and nourishing your immune system.

7. Kids need a supportive family culture. Sense of family identity e.g., Crazy family that camps…

8. Dinner table is where family members commiserate over skinned knees and snubs on the playground and not making the cut for

sports teams. It's also where families mark milestones, share dreams, bury sibling grudges, make compromises, celebrate successes, plan vacations, and tell jokes.

9. Dinner table is where kids learn the lessons that families teach: manners, cooperation, communication, self-control, values. Following directions. Sitting still. Taking turns. It's where kids learn to be part of a family and how to parent their own.'

10. Research**Dinner is the best predictor of how kids will do in adolescence," said Vijay. "Research has shown that the more frequently kids eat dinner with their families, the better they do in school, and the less likely they are to become sexually active, suffer depression, get involved with drugs or alcohol, or consider suicide.

11. Have healthy snacks and sit for ten minutes before preparing meal.

12. Not the food but conversation that is important. Keep it simple on week days. Let kids take turns helping plan and prepare menu. Rest clean up after.

13. On week-ends plan next week's meals as a family. Make desserts for lunches and freeze. Package chili, casseroles and freeze for week ahead.

14. Weekly idea: Open home for Kids' and friends' night.

CHAPTER EIGHT: BUILD YOUR HOUSE

15. Home is not a showplace. It's a place where people live!!

16. Make a game out of getting kids to eat, get to the car in time, pick up toys, get ready for bed...

17. Play with your kids—burns off their excess energy and energizes you.

18. Role play or use stuffed animals to act out traumatic events.

As Lilly wrote the final point, the audience began to clap. Cindy blushed.

"Well, I think that gives you your answer," said Lilly.

"May I have a copy of those notes?" asked one voice.

"Me too!" another added.

"I think we'd all like a copy," said Vijay, "if you don't mind, Cindy?"

"I am flattered," said Cindy. "Just leave me your email addresses and I'll see you get them."

The crowd departed dropping off cards and scraps of paper containing e-mail addresses.

TAKE A SIP

Now it's your turn!

1. What are some ways that you can bring fun and structure into your home?

2. What are some things you can do as a family weekly?

3. How can you make your home inviting for your family?

4. What routines can you establish so that your home runs smoothly?

5. Is your home a safe haven? If not, how can you make it one?

CHAPTER EIGHT: BUILD YOUR HOUSE

Notes:

Chapter Nine:
Family Is Everything

> You don't choose your family.
> They are God's gift to you,
> as you are to them.
> **~Desmond Tut**

With a gasp, Clarisse looked at Cindy. "You are a picture of the ultimate bride, Cindy," she said. "Derek is going to be speechless when you walk down that aisle."

Derek's girls, resplendent in pink lace, paused in their practice of sprinkling rose petals to stare at the newest member of their family. "You're like a fairy princess," Pamela breathed.

"Cinderella," Becky whispered.

"Well I guess it's unanimous," said Clarisse. "Come on, girls!" she called. "We've got some rose petals to scatter."

Straightening Cindy's veil, she whispered, "You've made an old lady very proud to be your matron of honor. See you at the altar."

Almost in a dream Cindy walked down the aisle on the arm of her father. At the altar, her dad raised her veil, kissed her gently, and whispered, "I prayed I'd live to see this day. Be happy, my darling. You've got a wonderful new family."

Quietly Mr. Matthew place Cindy's hand in Derek's, murmured, "Look after my little girl," and stepped back to join his tearful wife.

Clarisse took Cindy's bouquet and bent to retrieve the rings from the little girls' baskets.

When Cindy awoke the next morning, two bright little faces were staring at her, their blue eyes twinkling. Derek and Cindy had decided a winter honeymoon for the four of them was better than an immediate honeymoon for the two of them. Then Derek protested Cindy pointed out that she had married the three of them—not just him—and the girls did not need to experience a separation from their father so soon after losing their mother.

The day passed quickly. Cindy was putting in long hours at the veterinary clinic as a veterinary assistant. She had one more year to complete and she'd reach her career goal. So far, she'd gotten high marks at school and rave reviews from the pet owners at the clinic. At home she was busy being a mom and a wife. Her life was full of

CHAPTER NINE: FAMILY IS EVERYTHING

volunteering at the school where Becky was in kindergarten and Pamela in grade two. She was head of the PTA fund-raising committee to raise enough for new playground equipment. The figure skating club had convinced her to resurrect her sewing machine, dust off her sewing skills, and help create costumes for the club's figure skating carnival. She was a block parent and recently became a Brownie den mother.

With a little nudging from the ever-helpful Clarisse, she and Derek were taking the girls to Pastor Mike's church where they were both involved in choir and Sunday school.

When Derek suggested Cindy needed to make time for visits with Clarisse, Cindy readily agreed that she had been so busy since the wedding that she'd barely had time to visit with her friend.

"You are looking wonderful," Cindy observed smiling at her friend as she scooped up a spoonful of her fruit salad. "It's been too long since we last got together."

"You've been busy," Clarisse commented.

"Yes we have," agreed Cindy. We so appreciate your sitting with the girls until one of us gets home. Since it is hardly ever me first, I wanted to tell you the girls look forward to spending time with their Grandma Clarisse. It almost seems as if it is history repeating itself. It feels like only yesterday you and I were making cookies after school. The girls are so lucky to have you in their lives. I only hope you won't catch either of them sneaking out their bedroom window."

"I love spending time with the girls, Cindy. They make me feel young and needed. I am glad I can be a surrogate grandmother to them since their grandmothers are gone."

"Me too, Clarisse. I learned so many good lessons from you. I want my girls to have that experience."

"And they shall," agreed Clarisse. "But, let's talk about you," she said, eyeing her friend critically. "You look as if you've been drawn through a knot hole. Are you getting enough sleep?"

"Things have been very busy at work," admitted Cindy. "Then there's the house. I am finding it takes a lot longer to clean and do laundry now that we are four. Who knew two little girls could create such a mess in minutes? Then there's cooking and grocery shopping. And we have the girls in a lot of activities."

"What are you doing for yourself?" asked Clarisse.

"Well, I'm chair of the PTA fundraising committee. I volunteer at the school and I'm a new Brownie den mother."

"But what are you doing to look after yourself?" Clarisse persisted.

"Well," Cindy hedged, "by the time I get everything done at home and work, there doesn't seem to be a lot of time left."

"Just what I thought," said Clarisse. "So I have a great idea."

"Somehow I thought you would," said Cindy.

CHAPTER NINE: FAMILY IS EVERYTHING

"I called your doctor and she can see you at two this afternoon."

"But..." Cindy protested.

"No buts," insisted Clarisse. "Derek is looking after the girls and we have the afternoon to look after you."

Dr. McLennan looked at Cindy over her reading glasses as she studied the results of Cindy's lab work.

"When was your last period?" she asked.

"Before the wedding," responded Cindy.

"That was nine weeks ago," the doctor observed.

"Life has been hectic and I've never been regular," Cindy defended. "Is something wrong?" Cindy said in a worried voice.

"Well, the tests did show something has changed," Dr. McLennan said.

"Is it serious?" Cindy asked, her voice quavering.

"Well life-changing," the doctor clarified. She paused while Cindy held her breath. "You're pregnant, Cindy."

The remaining weeks of Cindy's pregnancy passed in a flash. Other than feeling tired all the time and always hungry,

Cindy was the picture of health. Derek and the girls just couldn't do enough for her. The girls set the table, made their beds and cleaned up their rooms without being nagged. At night, Derek rubbed her swelled feet and applied vitamin E cream to her stretch marks. He went out any time of the day or night in search of her favorite snacks: sardines, bagels and lox, and Jamoca Almond Fudge ice cream.

They talked into the night about baby names and hospital versus home delivery. The day that Cindy's ultrasound showed she was having a girl, she and Derek decided the baby would be named Clarisse…Baby Claire for short. To appease Derek's worries she agreed to have a hospital birth and Derek agreed to a midwife as long as an obstetrician was on call.

Cindy's water broke at 4 a.m. while Derek slept peacefully. When the pains were five minutes apart, Cindy called her midwife who said she'd meet her at the hospital. When she woke Derek, he bolted from the bed and grabbed his clothes, nearly tripping as he struggled into his pants.

Cindy quietly informed Clarisse, who had been sleeping over for the last week, that she and Derek were on the way to the hospital. "We'll call as soon as there is any news," she said as she steered the frazzled Derek to the car.

Baby Claire was born four hours after they arrived at the hospital. It was as easy a birth as it had been a pregnancy. The baby had fine black hair and pretty brown eyes like her sisters. She latched easily for nursing and slept quietly between feedings.

CHAPTER NINE: FAMILY IS EVERYTHING

Cindy was napping when a little giggle awoke her. Two pairs of dancing brown eyes stared at her. "Did you see your sister?" Cindy asked pointing to the cradle where the baby lay sleeping.

"Yes we did," said Pamela.

"But Clarisse said we couldn't touch her cause we'd wake her," Becky said softly.

"Well, it's just about time for her next feeding so you can touch her," Cindy said.

Two pairs of hands reached carefully into the cradle from either side. Tiny hands curled around their fingers. "Oh!" both girls exclaimed.

"What are we going to call her?" asked Pamela, always the more practical.

"We named her Clarisse," said Cindy, "but you can call her Baby Claire."

"That's a good name," said Becky. "She looks like a Baby Claire."

"I think so too," agreed Cindy. "We named her after her godmother."

"That's good," pronounced Becky. "Everyone should have a fairy godmother."

As the adults laughed, a single tear slid down Clarisse's cheek.

The weeks flew by in a jumble of summer camp for the girls, feeding and diapering and loads and loads of wash for Cindy. Suddenly, it was September and the girls were heading back to school. The summer, Baby Claire's christening, and the girls' birthdays had all flashed by.

The long autumn days stretched gloriously in front of Cindy. With the girls in school, she was able to take Baby Claire for long walks, often ending with coffee at Clarisse's.

With time to nap when Baby Claire did and to get household chores done during the day, Cindy regained her strength quickly. Her family returned home to nutritious, home-cooked meals and the smell of baking bread.

"I could get used to this," Derek murmured.

"Well, don't grow too accustomed to it," quipped Cindy. "My last year of veterinary school starts in January."

"Have you thought about what you're going to do with Baby Claire when you go back to school?" Clarisse asked Cindy one day just before Thanksgiving.

"The university has a great nursery program run by the Early Childhood Education students as part of their program. I've reserved a spot for her there. I can even go down on my lunch hour and play with her. The older girls are in school full time and we've enrolled them in the before and after school program. They are delighted to be with their friends."

CHAPTER NINE: FAMILY IS EVERYTHING

"I'm cooking Thanksgiving dinner next week," announced Clarisse. "I'd love to have you come and visit with my daughter Sandra."

"Sandra's coming from San Diego?" asked Cindy.

"Well Sandra is actually coming from San Antonio," said Clarisse. "Her company has opened a branch there and she is in charge of start-up."

"It will be nice to see her again. Why don't you and she come here? My mom and dad are flying in from The Villages. You can get caught up with them. My dad often asks about Clarisse-to-the-rescue. I finally convinced them to come and see the baby. Like all seniors who move to The Villages they seem to believe life outside The Villages has ceased to be important."

"Only if you let me make the pumpkin pies," said Clarisse

"Deal!" said Cindy.

༄

Thanksgiving dinner was a noisy affair as nine of them gathered around the table.

Before they dug into the delicious turkey Derek had cooked on the barbecue, Pamela asked if they could all say what they were thankful for.

"Me first!" piped up Becky. "I'm thankful for my new baby sister, Baby Claire and my big sister, Pamela……most of the time."

"I'm thankful for my new mommy and my daddy and my new sister……and my bratty little sister…..most of the time."

"And I am thankful for my new family and this beautiful house, and this delicious meal and to be able to shares it with all of the people who are dear to me," said Cindy.

"I'm thankful for people to share Thanksgiving Day with and to be out of the San Antonio traffic," said Sandra.

"I'm thankful to be sharing dinner with young people," said Cindy's dad. "The average age at The Villages is ninety-five!"

"You do have a point, dear," agreed Cindy's mom. If we'd had Thanksgiving dinner at the Community Center we'd have had to puree the turkey."

"Well I'm thankful for my girls—all four of them—and for a comfortable home and a job I enjoy."

"I am thankful for the love of all those with whom I am sharing this meal. You are all dear to me. I am such a lucky woman. And I'm thankful the pumpkin pies set!" said Clarisse.

"And God bless everyone," said Pamela and Becky in unison.

The phone rang late the next morning.

Cindy reached for it, thinking about her parents who had flown back to The Villages that morning.

CHAPTER NINE: FAMILY IS EVERYTHING

"Hello Cindy. This is Sandra Caldwell. Mom died in her sleep last night. When she wasn't up by ten I went to wake her. She was lying there a book on her chest like she'd just drifted off to sleep."

"Oh, no!" said Cindy. "I can't believe she's gone. I thought she'd outlive us all."

"Cindy, she was ninety-eight," said Sandra. "She lived a wonderful, happy life. And you were a good part of it. Do you have any idea how pleased she was to be your Matron of Honor and Baby Claire's namesake and godmother?"

"Would you say a few words at her funeral? You were her dearest friend."

"Of course," said Cindy.

In a daze, she hung up to give Derek the news.

Take a Sip

Family, Family, Family

1. Has your family circle been broken by unforgiveness? If so, how can you help fix it?

2. Do you regularly show the people you love that you appreciate them? If not, how can you start?

4. Take some time TODAY to tell someone you love them.

5. Be the change you want to see.

CHAPTER NINE: FAMILY IS EVERYTHING

Notes:

Epilogue

"Why did you do all this for me?" he asked.
"I don't deserve it. I've never done anything for you."
"You have been my friend," replied Charlotte.
"That in itself is a tremendous thing."
~E.B. White

With a catch in her throat, Cindy looked at the hundreds of individuals who had gathered to pay a final tribute to Clarisse Caldwell. She began to speak. Her voice quavered at first and then grew stronger.

"Somehow I never dreamed this day would come. I thought our dearest friend, Clarisse, would live forever—like that mighty oak in her front yard. I cannot begin to imagine my life without her. For, you see, Clarisse has always been there for me. She was the one who ratted me out when, as a hormone-ridden teen, I used to sneak out my bedroom window. It was Clarisse who got me into Abbotsford School for Girls where I learned the importance of a good education. It was Clarisse who pulled strings to get me into a world-famous drug rehab program where I learned that being a meth addict was not how I wanted to live my life. Clarisse helped me sort out my calling in life. She helped me get into a co-op and, consequently, a good veterinary school. Clarisse had connections everywhere.

"When I doubted my ability to be a good wife and mother, Clarisse always had the right resource people and courses that just happened have an opening.

"I've heard some amazing stories of how Clarisse befriended so many of you at a time when you badly needed a good friend. I have no idea how she found time for you. I thought I was her full-time project. Whenever I was down, Clarisse lifted me up. When I doubted myself, Clarisse was always there to build my confidence and nudge me forward. I would not be the happy wife and mother I am today if Clarisse had not been in my life. Clarisse was a great friend. She was the kind of friend that stands by you when you need somebody to be there. Clarisse saved my life.

"What is it that we will remember when we think of Clarisse? I think everyone who knew her very well will remember how Clarisse interfered with the course of our lives and made them better. Clarisse was my closest friend, my matron of honor, Baby Claire's godmother, our girls' beloved Fairy Godmother, and my greatest cheerleader.

"When I asked Clarisse why she bothered with me when I was such an ungrateful pain, she answered that I was her calling. She quoted the famous words of E. B. White in Charlotte's Web when Wilbur asked her why she bothered with him, noting that he'd never done anything for

EPILOGUE

the spider. Charlotte answered: "You have been my friend. That in itself is a tremendous thing."

Most of us are here today to pay last tribute to Clarisse because we were lucky enough to be recipients of that "tremendous thing" that was Clarisse's friendship.

"Clarisse was a great believer in paying it forward. I promise to pay forward the great gift of friendship that Clarisse gave me. It will be my calling to continue her legacy and meddle—for good—in as many lives as I can.

"Clarisse always wanted to make people happy. Her death was sudden. I remember when I heard the news I simply could not believe it. After all, I always expected that Clarisse would be there to help Derek and me raise our daughters—just as she had helped my parents. Clarisse was so successful in her creative interventions that my dad took to calling this wonderful woman Clarisse-to-the-rescue.

"Clarisse lived her life wonderfully. She was well-loved by everyone she met and I have no doubt she's up there at God's right hand helping Him sort things out in Heaven.

"I will forever be grateful to have known Clarisse. I feel eternally blessed that

Clarisse was always there at the right place and at the right time to bail me out and enrich my life. From Clarisse, I learned to trust the words of A. A. Milne: 'Promise me you'll always remember: You're braver than you believe, and stronger than you seem, and smarter than you think.'

"Clarisse will forever live in my heart…In our hearts. Anne of Green Gables said, 'True friends are always together in spirit.' So, my friend, Clarisse, you shall always live on.

"This is not the time for us to grieve her death. Clarisse would want us to celebrate her life. Let the sharing begin."

EPILOGUE

Take a Sip

How would you like to be remembered?

Notes

www.ingramcontent.com/pod-product-compliance
Lightning Source LLC
LaVergne TN
LVHW051123080426
835510LV00018B/2195